I'M GOING TO THE TOP

D1051420

JOHN HAREMZA

with Peter Lees

I'm Going To The Top

Pride Publishing, A Division of Sound Concepts

500 South Geneva Road

Vineyard, UT 84058

ISBN 1-887938-52-4

How to Order

Copies may be ordered from Sound Concepts,

500 S. Geneva Rd., Vineyard, UT 84058; telephone (888) 507-3925.

Visit us online at www.soundconcepts.com/rexall

John has been and continues to be not only an inspiration to distributors but also a significant catalyst to the Rexall's total success. His I can and I will attitude say it all. Our journey "to the top" has just started. Let John and his story inspire you to create the new chapters in your book. Whether you're just starting or five, ten or twenty chapters along you choose the remaining chapters. Its your story to write. Make your best seller a reality

Damon DeSantis President & CEO Rexall Sundown
CEO Rexall Showcase International

There is no road to success that is free from obstacles. We will all incur them and some will incur more than others. To each of us these obstacles look different but they're still there. While most people quit when they reach these obstacles those who face the most obstacles and overcome them are those who serve as an inspiration to all of us. I would like to congratulate John as someone who overcame these obstacles and did not make excuses. Thanks John.

Todd Smith, PBOA
Presidential Triple Diamond Director, Century Club,

John Haremza is one of the most inspirational people I know. His story of overcoming obstacles and refining himself is an inspiration to anyone who listens to it. This book captures perfectly his story and allows people to be able to enjoy and reread in their own moments of difficulty about a person who overcame severe challenges. I recommend this book to everyone who wants to make a better person out of themselves. Put me down for the first 100 off the press.

Stewart Hughes,
Triple Diamond Director, Century Club, PBOA

The John Haremza story is ultimately about having the desire to achieve the impossible dream. John has confronted adversity head on and I am amazed at his ability to overcome adversity and to maintain his I can attitude. His story has been and will continue to be inspirational for thousands of individuals within and outside of Rexall Showcase International. I am truly blessed to have John as a top leader within our organization.

David Scofield, President, Rexall Showcase International

John Haremza has not only captured the essence of success with Rexall Showcase International, he has captured the foundation of success in life. John's story brings tears to your eyes, a proven formula for attaining our RSI goals, and the absolute example that we can all reach the "top"!

Gordon Oswald,
Triple Diamond Director, Century Club, PBOA

John Haremza shows great sensitivity, insight and wisdom in "I'm Going to the Top". Aside from being a true inspiration, his practical insights will help any distributor achieve their own goals in a timely fashion. I believe this book will be a true asset to everyone.

Janie Fischer,
Triple Diamond Director, Century Club, PBOA

John Haremza is an inspiration for how achievable business success, personal fulfillment and happiness are in this land of opportunity. He is also an example and a role model for quality men and women who might otherwise squander their lives. "I'm Going to the Top" is a must read for anyone who has not achieved their dreams and has a desire to do something about it.

Jim Moyles,
Triple Diamond Director, Century Club, PBOA

The rags to riches rise of John Haremza in Rexall Showcase and the network marketing industry is one of the most compelling and exciting stories in the history of US business. John proves to one and all that our lives are limited only by the barriers we place in front of ourselves. We will all be at the top in Rexall if we believe that we can, and take the necessary action.

David Bailly, Century Club

I have known John Haremza for many years now but after learning of the obstacles John has overcome I have gained even more respect for the man. John's unique humor and detailed instruction make this one of the best books on how to be successful in network marketing that I have ever read.

Gary Mooers, Triple Diamond Director, PBOA

Wow! Unbelievable! This is one of the finest reads in network marketing. It illustrates what the business can be, what it can do for people, and what the possibilities are. I thought it was great.

Doug Overvold, Triple Diamond Director, Century Club

I really enjoyed reading John's book. This is a true portrayal of the American dream. Given the right opportunity and the right environment every one of us can accomplish our objectives regardless of our handicaps or obstacles. John's story is living proof that we can make it 'to the top'. This book will inspire you to go for greatness.

Jeff Mack, Triple Diamond Director, Century Club

John, I just finished reading your manuscript. It is deeply insightful, very motivating and inspirational. It proves that if you have the desire you can accomplish anything. I was very impressed.

Janet Bloom, Triple Diamond Director, Century Club

John's constant commitment to winning has been an inspiration to each and every one of us. We all admire his focus, discipline and perseverance in building his Rexall Showcase International business.

John Berta, Most Valuable Leader,
Triple Diamond Director, Century Club

I really enjoyed John's book on my way to Japan. This is the book that anyone who has ever heard John's story has wanted to see published. It's an inspiring tale of how, with a deep enough vision, anything can come true.

Eddie Stone,
Triple Diamond Director, Century Club, PBOA

John's story is an inspiration to all of those who feel as if they have had the deck in life stacked against them and are still looking to succeed. It is truly a compelling story.

Tom Bissmeyer,
Triple Diamond Director, Century Club, PBOA

Based on my seven years in this industry, I felt that honesty was the greatest attribute of John's book. I know that we would all love to have a person-to-person, heart-to-heart discussion with a national leader in one of the top network marketing companies. That is the opportunity John gives you in his book. It is your place and your time to have your own personal and intimate conversation with John. He shares his experiences and what he has learned in the business so that we can all benefit from it. This is just like the real John.

Renee Stewart Chittick,
Triple Diamond Director, Century Club, PBOA

What a compelling story of resiliency, perseverance and grass roots leadership! A master storyteller, John inspires you to attain huge success.

Dr. Neal Secrist,

Air Force Flight Surgeon, Emergency Physician

This is a wonderful book, full of inspiration and motivation It will help you reach your dreams.

Brian Tracy, Author of Maximum Achievement, and

of my favorite tape sets including, Getting Rich in

America, the Luck Factor and the Psychology of Success

If you're looking for proof that personal development is the key to success, look no further. John Haremza's odyssey from Maintenance Manager to Millionaire is the classic American success story. It has all the elements of a great saga. From a trailer park to a home on the most expensive lake in Minnesota, from wanting to be invisible in high school to celebrity status with Rexall Showcase, from a subsistence wage to one of the top earners in the industry, John's story is a must read. It is an example of courage for each and every one of us. Imagine living with a disability like dyslexia, being put down and made to feel stupid in front of your friends and still having the courage to go door-to-door, all alone, in the middle of winter. Congratulations John, on your book, on your story, on your courage, on your success. You are an inspiration.

Bob Proctor, one of North America's premier motivational

speakers and a leader in the field of personal development.

I'm Going to the Top is a must read book that will encourage and inspire you in your journey to success. I'm confident you'll find this book a very valuable investment of your time. I know that I did.

Ben Kubassek, Author of Succeed Without Burnout

I _____

am going to the top.

_____
Date

Foreword by Randy Schroeder

John Haremza is one who has shown the tenacity and strength to overcome obstacles in his personal life as well as one who has demonstrated the ability to grow professionally to points of success beyond that which his former peers could imagine. Having emerged from a humble and challenging background John is now in a unique position to teach us all about the various facets of success: tenacity, perseverance, a never quit attitude and a willingness to push himself harder than anyone else would ever push him. I consider myself lucky to call John a friend and invite you to immerse yourself in the success concepts taught in this book. Invest an hour or two in your success. Read and reread this text and put the proven principles to work in your life. I wish you the best in your personal quest for success.

Randy Schroeder, PBOA
Presidential Triple Diamond Director, Century Club,

Introduction by Dr. Louis Pack

We have all heard various rags to riches stories, but to personally know someone such as John who epitomizes such a transformation is just remarkable. His rise from true "blue collar Americana" in the face of financial hardships, peer skepticism and an incredible learning disability is the kind of stuff Hollywood movies are made of.

I know the meaning of hard work. Anyone who becomes a surgeon does. Having always had reading disabilities of my own, (my early claim to fame was being Chairman of the Remedial Reading Group), I can only imagine how hard this journey has been for John.

John Haremza has truly been transformed. Not by a stroke of luck or the helping hand of a caretaker, but by the power of his sheer will, the most powerful of all human traits. Who among us would ever have believed that he was capable of attaining true success let alone mastering it?

"I'm Going to the Top" is John Haremza's vivid journey of personal triumph. It is inspirational, heart warming and meaningful to us all. If it were nothing more than this, every line would still be worth reading. Yet this book doesn't stop there. John, having mastered this industry just like he did his last, shares in very specific terms his secrets of success in our industry of network marketing. He covers motivation, strategy, goal setting and other key aspects of the business, providing a cook book approach to developing a successful distributorship.

"I'm Going to the Top" is a great story about a super guy and a wonderful business. It should only happen to each and every one of us!

Dr. Louis Pack

> *I look at challenges as mountains.*
> *I have dedicated this book to those rare*
> *individuals who are determined to*
> *scale their own mountains.*

This book is dedicated to those individuals who have made a personal commitment that; "they are going to the top". To those who have decided that they will confront and overcome the challenges of life and the challenges we face in network marketing. They have determined that they are going to the top of the mountain. You may find them dead along the side, but you will not find them at the bottom of the mountain.

I'm Going to the Top

You will find me at the top of the mountain or dead along the side.

John Haremza

With Peter Lees

Please understand that individual results vary and different people experience different results from these Rexall Showcase International products as well as from this business opportunity. No guarantees expressed or implied are made in this book. The discussion of various potential benefits to be derived from using these products or participating in this business are not meant as guarantees. Also this book is not a substitute for medical advice. You should consult your physician before beginning any diet, supplementation or regarding any medical symptoms.

TABLE OF CONTENTS

Introduction by John Haremza

Why would a guy who can't read a book, write a book? This question is particularly relevant when telling the story brings back such painful memories.

The answer is I believe my story empowers others. It can give hope to anyone who is facing major challenges in life. I look at challenges as mountains. Let's face it, network marketing brings with it a whole new set of challenges. When I first got involved in network marketing I felt as if I was facing not just a challenge, not just one mountain but a range of mountains.

My major challenge is that I have been handicapped with severe dyslexia. What you do with such ease is beyond my reach. To this day I cannot pick up a book or a newspaper and read it. This disability created serious challenges for me all through my school years and my early working years.

Confronting this mountain gave me the determination to succeed whatever the obstacle; it gave me the determination to "go to the top".

It is my hope that you will find that this book brings out the resources you have deep within yourself, resources that will take you "to the top".

Thank You

I want to start by thanking all those people who told me that I could not be a success in network marketing, the ones who told me I should stay at my nice safe maintenance job and be content. I know that this advice was well intentioned, but nevertheless they told me that I could not do it and that gave me the determination to make it happen, and to show them that they were wrong.

To my wife, Jana who has stood by me through the tough times of getting started and to my children Stephanie and Nicole thank you for your patience. To my parents who have been so supportive, thank you. Dad, I'm not sure where I would be today if you had not believed in me enough to co-sign that first note that got me into network marketing.

Todd Smith has been an excellent leader and the most influential person in my network-marketing career. Thank you Todd for convincing me along with Cliff and Doug Overvold that Rexall Showcase was the right place to be. Your coaching and leadership laid the foundations for our success in Rexall Showcase.

Todd Smith, Randy Schroeder and Stewart Hughes demonstrated a caliber of leadership that both inspired me and kept me on track through my career with Rexall Showcase. I owe a great deal to them for their vision and their leadership.

Cliff and Doug Overvold have been my partners through this journey, their support and companionship have never wavered.

Thank you Peter Lees for suggesting that we write this book and for convincing me that others would be empowered by my story.

I appreciate the contributions of Dr. Lou Pack, Martin Kochberg, Gem Morris, Neil Roth, and Cindy Rich for their review, editing and suggestions.

My front line directors Claire and Neil Roth, Al and Jane Johnson, Doug and Sue Overvold, Cindy and Tim Rich, Chuck and Patty Hendricks, Ray and Emanuela Agrusta have been the driving force in my organization. Thank you.

This book would not have been published without the support and assistance of Sound Concepts.

The home team at Rexall Showcase made this story possible for me and for the thousands of us that believe we can make a positive difference in the lives of others. Damon DeSantis, President Rexall Sundown and David Schofield, President Rexall Showcase are leaders that we can take pride in.

I am convinced that I would still be a maintenance manager if it had not been for the inspiration of speakers such as Zig Ziglar, Jim Rohn, Lou Tice, Brian Tracy and Anthony Robbins. It was Zig Ziglar's flea story that got me out of the jar.

No acknowledgment would be complete without mention of my organization. I am convinced that I have the best organization in the industry. Without each and every one of you there would be no John Haremza story. Thank you.

The Story Behind the Story:

John's story gives hope to many of us in network marketing, it empowers us. If John could overcome his challenges to become one of the leaders in Rexall Showcase then there is hope for all of us. We too can overcome the challenges we face.

For four solid days, at John's lake home, with a tape recorder going, I asked him all the questions a new distributor would ask. We taped his answers and they became the content of this book.

We divided the book into four sections. The first section is the story of John's journey from maintenance manager to millionaire, section two is the milestones we as distributors should watch for on our journey, the third section is designed to take a potential distributor through the sponsoring and getting started cycle, and section four looks at the rewards of the journey and where we go from here.

It has been a pleasure working with John to get his story in print.

Peter Lees

The Journey from Maintenance Manager to Millionaire

Facing the challenges of life.

How large is your dream?

Dealing with dream stealers.

The question is, "Will you get up?"

"You can get anything you want in life if you just help enough other people get what they want."

Zig Ziglar

---

*Work harder on yourself than you
work on your job.
When you work on your job, you
make a living,
when you work on yourself,
you'll make a fortune."*
Jim Rohn

CHAPTER 1

The Dream Begins

How did you first hear about network marketing? Who introduced you to the concept?

I remember it as if it was yesterday. Dan Sweere, a good friend invited me to his house on a Wednesday evening to take a look at a new water filter business he was considering. Being a Maintenance Manager, I assumed that he wanted me to check the product over to see if it was well built, give him some advice, possibly build a display – something of that nature. Unfortunately the usual happened that evening. When you're in maintenance, you're on call all the time. Things can happen and much of the work has to be done off-peak hours when the production lines are shut down. Instead of getting off work at 5:00 we had a serious problem with one of our production lines and I was still at the plant at 8:30 working with my crew. By the time I got to Dan's house it was after 9:00. I walked in, two hours late, in my blue work clothes, with grease from head to toe. We wore hairnets because of the food environment and I still had mine on along with my glasses that were the protective type with shields on the side.

As I walked in I was introduced to two guys in suits from Minneapolis. I could hear them thinking; "We just waited two hours to talk to this guy?" I lived in a little town of about 2,000 people, 250 miles from Minneapolis. These two business guys had come down from Minneapolis to present the business to me and five or six of my buddies. They must have been shaking their heads in disbelief at what they saw. They had come 250 miles to this town in the middle of nowhere, in the middle of winter to meet with a maintenance manager!

The first thing they did was a test. This was on a lake in the country and water was brown and rusty. They hooked a filter up and the water went from tasting terrible, almost undrinkable, to as clear as a bell and it tasted good. My response was, "I need one of these, everyone needs one of these." These guys were good, they could tell the story and I got excited. As a matter of fact, we were all excited. I bought four water filters on the spot. I wrote out a check for $420.00 and told them to hold the check until Friday when I got paid.

This was November 1988, I was getting married in December. I walked in at midnight to show my fiancee the load of water filters that I just bought. She was, needless to say, very upset. We were planning to get married, money was tight and her first question was "How much did they cost?" I told her, "$420.00, but don't worry; they're going to hold the check till the end of the week." We were in debt and here I am spending money we didn't have.

Now this is the best part of the story.

Jana was very upset. I said, "Honey, wait till you see what this thing does." I hooked the water filter up, ran the water and it did not change a thing, the water looked and tasted just like it always looked and tasted. The water we had in town was actually fairly good water. It wasn't chlorinated, tasted fine, and the filter did not change the water at all. Jana's response was "I can see that these filters are going to go over well." I was still excited so I went on to tell her that it took $5,000 to get involved in the business and I was going to invest the $5,000. Now she was convinced that I had gone off the deep end, but she was relieved because she knew that I could never come up with the money.

It was November and we were living in a 12 x 70, 1969 Garland trailer house. This was an old trailer house with 2 x 2 walls. These trailers used newspaper in the walls for insulation. The frost would come two feet up the walls on the inside of the trailer. You could scrape frost off the walls if you wanted to put it in a drink, that's the type of frost I'm talking about. We had a natural gas furnace but something was wrong with it and we didn't have the money to get it repaired. A few times a day the pilot would blow out and then it would backfire and blow the cover off the furnace against the wall. I'd have to come home from work to re-light the furnace. It was an interesting life and then I roll in at midnight and announce that I'm going to invest $5,000 in water filters, into some "scam" as Jana believed it to be. No wonder she was skeptical. This was more than my old trailer was worth.

Jana talked to my parents, her parents, her brother-in-law, anybody, and everybody trying to get them to convince me that I had lost my mind. I know that she did it with the best of intentions, with real concern for our welfare. By now everybody could see that I was committed, my father-in-law thought for sure that I was going to put us in the poor house. Finally as a last resort, Jana said, "I'm not going to marry you if you do it", I said, "Do what you've got to do, but I'm going to do this."

I could not articulate it at the time but I believe it is far less damaging to a relationship to try and to fail than to live with the resentment of never trying at all. If I had seen others succeed at network marketing and never tried myself, I would never have been able to forgive Jana or myself. A negative spouse can be a major hurdle in network marketing. About four months later it was Jana who encouraged me to go full time.

When Jana saw that I was still determined she said, "OK, fine, do it, but let's get our bills paid off first." I said, "Honey, at the rate we're going, that's going to take 15 to 20 years, provided we don't incur any more debt. I'm looking to do this to make money – not spend money."

So I went ahead and did it. I got my dad to co-sign a note for me, reluctantly, and I bought 40 water filters.

Now the story gets better still.

The water filters showed up the same week we got married. This did not sit well, the tension was high. I took a week off work after we got married. Most couples would have gone on a honeymoon but we didn't have the money so I went out to sell water filters door-to-door.

---

*I believe that it is far better to try and to fail than
to live with the resentment of never trying at all.*

We got married December 17, so this was the 20th of December, right before Christmas. I had no understanding of network marketing so I started knocking on doors, going door-to-door, trying to sell water filters. My hometown of Perham had good water so I went to another town 45 minutes away. We used the "puppy-dog close". If you could get someone to try a filter they would see the difference in their water and they would want to keep it.

Here comes this kid, knocking on your door, wearing nothing but slacks and a shirt. Probably jeans and a shirt, I don't think I owned slacks back then. My tie used to go halfway down my shirt. I had no coat, I think people let me in just out of kindness and courtesy.

The first time I went to town, I drove around for two hours, trying to decide what to do, getting my nerve up. If there were two cars in the driveway, I thought they must have company, so I wouldn't call on them. If there was one car in the driveway, I thought, well they're probably both not home and I'd want them both to be there so I wouldn't call on them. I made up every excuse possible not to knock on those doors, but I did it. I had to do it. I could not go home with all those filters. I had no one behind me. What I did have was a lot of pressure on me with everybody saying this wasn't going to work. Sometimes I think I should go back and thank every one of them for telling me that I could not do it. That's probably what gave me the determination to make it happen. I had burned my bridges behind me and that gave me the courage to knock on all those doors.

Courage is resistance to fear, mastery of fear.
It is not the absence of fear.
Mark Twain

That first day, I got three people to try a filter.

My brother was curious so I took him with me the following week. We went back to the three homes where I had placed a water filter and I sold one of them. I made $59 right on the spot. I bought it for $120, sold it for $179 and made $59 right there. My brother and I were ecstatic. "How could you make $59 so fast?" We thought that we were on our way to becoming rich!

Now my parents were really upset because I dragged my brother into this and he bought $5,000 worth of filters. He and I went out two to three times a week. We'd drive to this town after work and we would knock on doors, he would take one side of the street, I'd take the other. We would knock on doors and place water filters. We probably knocked on 200 doors and for the most part, everybody was nice and tried them. But we never sold another water filter.

Courage conquers fear.

ZIG ZIGLAR COMES TO TOWN:

While I was still working full time and doing network marketing on the side, I heard that Zig Ziglar was coming to Fargo. You can imagine the ribbing I took from my co-workers. "Hey John, have you seen that zig zag guy yet. That positive thinking stuff is all baloney. You're wasting your money". They laughed at me then. I guess they're still there - still laughing?

Zig got me on track to climb my second mountain to build myself, to build my self-esteem.

Zig told a story that inspired me. I'm convinced that his flea story got me out of the jar and on the road to a much brighter future. Zig said "If you take a fruit jar, fill it with fleas and put a lid on it those fleas will go crazy jumping, hitting their head on the lid trying to get out of the jar. Eventually their heads get sore, but because they like to jump they continue to jump but just high enough so they don't hit their head on the lid. You can take the lid off the jar and they'll never jump out. They have been conditioned to believe that they can't get out of the jar.

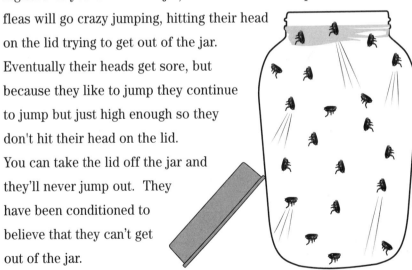

I believe that we have all been conditioned. We have been flea trained. Think of a baby, it has no fear, no limitations and no boundaries. This flea training begins when we are very young and is carried on through school and in our society. We're taught that we can't climb mountains.

What Zig did that day took me out of the jar. The combination of network marketing and Zig's flea story opened my eyes. I began to see that I could be more than a Maintenance Manager, more than the invisible man, more than someone afraid of his own shadow. I am greatly indebted to Zig for coming to Fargo that day.

To be successful in network marketing you must become a leader. Most new distributors do not have a belief structure within themselves. You need to be a life support system. You need to be their energy, their life support system. You need to be someone they can believe in. That is what I was, what I became, and what I am still becoming. As I fed myself people began to follow me.

With this experience behind you what made you decide to go full time into network marketing? You were doing OK as a Maintenance Manager, your supervisors appreciated you and your contributions. You had a job for life, your dream job. Why would you leave all of that?

You need to be the energy, the life support system of your distributors.

Zig Ziglar and John Haremza

That is the question that my family asked me many times over. "Why would you leave a good secure job where you are so well respected?"

Ultimately, it was one guy. Someone convinced me to go to a NSA meeting, the first network marketing meeting I ever attended. I'll never forget this guy, walking across the stage in a baseball hat, dented in at the front wearing bib overalls with one pant leg tucked into his boot and the other pant leg hanging out. Just to complete the picture he had manure on his boots. Looking back I think he was missing some teeth. He got up on stage and said he had made $10,000 just last month. I don't know what else was mentioned at that meeting, but I do remember that $10,000. That was when I said, "I can do this", and I became incredibly enthusiastic. I have heard it said, "If you set yourself on fire, people will travel for miles to watch you burn". That is exactly what was happening to me, I was on fire, I saw a way out and I was enthusiastic. People did not know what I was talking about but they wanted to join me because of my enthusiasm. Their response was, "I don't know what you're doing but I want to do it, too."

Going door-to-door is a tough way to get started in network marketing, what got you on the right track?

After I signed up I never heard from my sponsor again, I'm sure he thought I was just another statistic. One day I called him out of frustration and he told me that a Mike Nelson was doing a meeting in Fargo, about 60 miles from my hometown. Kevin Turnis, a friend, my brother, and I went to the meeting. We were going to listen to this guy, get motivated, excited and go knocking on doors again. Mike told us how we needed to recruit and sponsor other people. I thought, "Why in the world would I want to create my own competition?" All I could see was selling water filters; I couldn't see the leverage aspect of network marketing. Mike Nelson was very good, very motivating, so I talked to him after the meeting. I told him how I enjoyed his speech and we were heading out to knock on some doors. Mike said, "You know, I made $205,000 last year and if you told me I had to knock on doors I would not have done it." He asked, "Who's your sponsor?" When I told him who my sponsor was, he replied, "You're in my downline. Come up to my room after the next session."

We went up to Mike's room and he explained the recruiting aspects of the business. From that moment on I had a paradigm shift in the way I did business. I began to recruit. Now I could see that people got a whole lot more excited about making money than they did about spending it. When I talked about selling them a water filter they had to spend money. When I talked to them about cashing in on this major industry of water filtration and the direction it was headed they could see the opportunity. Instead of buying one filter for their own use, they would buy forty of them to do the business. It made a huge difference and I began to make some money.

Now my family, although they were still very upset, began to see a change in my attitude. I was so excited I barely slept. I worked from bell to bell. I would go to work at my maintenance job and the whole time I was there, my head was just spinning, thinking about all this stuff.

One day a week, I would take off early around 3:00 or 4:00, load up my car with prospects and head for the business briefing in Minneapolis 250 miles, four hours away. We would go the meeting, get charged up, be home at 2:00 a.m. and back to work the next morning. Every week I'd bring new people down there. People were feeding off of my energy. I began to realize that there was a future here. Now I could see it. The interesting thing was that Jana, my wife began to see it and she encouraged me to go full-time.

It was when I made the decision to go full-time that I got the real heat from my friends and co-workers. This was when the teasing and taunting started in earnest. To this day I can remember sitting in the break room with some of my co-workers. The consensus was that I would never make it and that it would never work for me.
The now famous break room.

There are a couple of negative people in this
world and they move around a lot.

The now famous break room.

"*Maybe you're right but the worst that can happen is that I'll have to come back and get a job like you've got.*"

My reply, and you could have heard a pin drop was, "Maybe you're right but the worst that can happen is that I'll have to come back and get a job like you've got."

My superiors were convinced that I had lost my mind. They called me into the office numerous times, saying, "John, what are you doing? You're throwing your life away. You have built a reputation; you have established yourself with this company. You've got a life-long job. We hate to see you throw it away." They were, I believe, doing this out of sincere concern for me. They never tried to discourage me as my co-workers did. They were trying to say, "Hey, we care about you, you are a valuable employee, an important member of the team, we want you to stay, you went over the deep end here, let's get you back under control. Let's get you back in the jar."

People will, with the best of intentions,
try to steer you off course, to nudge you off
course, to convince you off course, to distract
you off course. They will try to convince
you that you are dreaming.

My First Suit

I was asked to speak at a large meeting in Minneapolis. As we were driving down I was telling Jana that they wanted me to go on stage and tell my story. Here I was scheduled to speak to a thousand people and I didn't own a suit. We stopped in a town called St. Cloud and I bought a grey pinstripe suit. The meeting was Saturday morning and we were driving down on Friday. The clerk said, "No problem we'll have it ready for you tomorrow." That was not good enough. We had to have it right then and be on our way. Jana said, "I'll take care of it." She hemmed the pant legs and the sleeves with safety pins. There I was, telling my story for the first time, standing on the stage in front of a thousand people, wearing my first grey pinstripe suit, held together with safety pins.

The recognition felt great and so did the newcar.

There is little difference in people, but that little difference makes a big difference. The little difference is attitude.The big difference is whether it is positive or negative.

W.Clement Stone

Nothing can stop the man with the right mental attitude from achieving his goal. Nothing on earth can help the man with the wrong attitude.

Thomas Jefferson

The most significant change in a person's life is a change of attitude, right attitude produces right actions.

William J. Johnson

CHAPTER 2

The Early Years

John most of us know you from your video or from the stage as you do your presentations. We see you as a leader, as a well-dressed and articulate leader. It's hard to imagine you as a maintenance manager. Tell us about your early years.

As I think back to my early childhood I am reminded of the flea training story. I was like a flea in a fruit jar. I was always jumping, always trying new things trying to get out of the jar. From my earliest years I was ambitious.

My parents tell me when they were building their house we were living at my grandmother's house about two blocks down the road. At four years of age I would take off on my tricycle, cross a highway and tell the carpenters what to do. I was tough to control. I was energetic back then and I had a lot of confidence.

I was a pretty ambitious kid. I remember building birdhouses out of popsicle sticks and selling them to our neighbors. Most of them bought the birdhouses, probably just because I was a kid. I did make one mistake. I didn't use waterproof glue and the birdhouses fell apart when it rained. Nobody said anything or asked for their money back. I didn't offer the Rexall Showcase International 100% money-back guarantee in those days.

When I was a little older I started a garden tilling business. My dad had to drive me around. Eventually my older brother got his license and he drove me around. He wanted a piece of the action so I would sell people on our tilling service and he would do the work. How's that for leverage?

Here's another story that shows a little bit of my ambition. My dad had tried a lot of things and was an incredibly hard worker. He had been beaten down and finally settled for a regular job. He used to frustrate me because when somebody said they were going to do something, I took it for granted that they were going to do it. I remember him talking about putting patio doors in our kitchen. He kept talking about it and talking about it and talking about it. I must have been 14 when I came home one day and decided, today's the day, we're going to do the patio doors. I ripped out the window and cut the wall down to the floor. When mom and dad came home from work I was sitting there with the whole wall torn apart. Dad was a little upset, but we got the patio doors. We had no choice.

When we installed the patio doors I had to move an electrical plug and a water baseboard heater. I was very handy; my ultimate trade – my passion, at that point – was building, working with my hands. I was not perceived as being "smart".

It was around the same time period my parents were talking about building a sauna in our basement. One day I took it upon myself to begin building it. I got the project started and my dad had to finish it. It got to the point where my parents were afraid to tell me something because they knew if they told me I'd do it.

It was not until I started school that I faced the challenge of reading and began to get beaten down. I had severe dyslexia; I could not read. No matter now hard I tried, and believe me I tried, I could not read. When I tried to read all the words ran together. The assumption was that I was slow and stupid. Remember this was long before dyslexia was identified as a disability.

I often look back and think of dyslexia as a mountain, an invisible mountain. I could not see it. My parents, my friends, my teachers had no idea of the challenge I faced. To them it was an invisible mountain and their assumption was that I was just a dumb kid.

It was very, very frustrating for me and to everyone around me. They took me to the eye doctor to see if I needed glasses. My vision wasn't as good as it could have been and I did get glasses. I could see a little better but I still could not read. They tried all kinds of different things even having a ruler with a slot in it so I could see just one word at a time.

The frustration was not just with me. It was with everybody around me. My teachers wanted to know why I couldn't read, my parents wanted to know why I couldn't read, and I wanted to know why I couldn't read.

As you can imagine the feelings of inferiority were overwhelming. In some respect I hold my teachers responsible, but back then they didn't know any better. They thought I was slow or dumb or just not trying hard enough. When they called on me to read out loud in class I had to stumble through it. The embarrassment was unbelievable. It was not just my inability to read. It was also my classmates taunting me.

When we were reading out loud in class we would take turns reading a paragraph. I used to count ahead to guess which one I would be called on to read. I would practise and practise so that I would somehow get through it the best I could. Then they'd go and call on someone out of order and mess me up completely. Imagine feeling as low as you have ever felt. That's how I felt every day at school. Imagine being called out of class on every test so that the test could be read to you.

My parents knew how good I was with my hands but they were frustrated. I remember sitting in the garage one day and overhearing my dad telling one of his best friends how stupid I was and how he wondered what I was going to do in life. I crawled into the doghouse with my black lab Lady and cried. At least she understood me. If everybody had the passion and love that a dog has it would be a better world. Many such incidences occurred. The sad thing was that I began to believe that I was a slow, stupid kid.

Ultimately, it was determined that I would never be able read and that I should be taught enough to survive. I was put in special classes and taught the basics such as balancing a checkbook, reading a menu and reading signs.

Coming back to the flea training story that I spoke about, I think many of us are born with a lot of ambition. It was my school experience that beat me down to the point where I was afraid of my own shadow. This was the beginning of wanting to crawl into a shell and be invisible. Everything you do in school from academic subjects to sports to extra-curricular activities involves reading. I listened well, but I was afraid to speak up in class. I did not want to be seen because I might be called on to read and have to experience the embarrassment all over again.

I did an incredible job of masking my disability. Even as an adult my wife did not know that I could not read. My mother finally told her. Once she found out she began to put the pieces together. She said, "I used to get irritated with you when you would ask me to spell something or to, 'read this for me real quick'. I always wondered why, I was beginning to think you were just lazy". At work if someone handed me something to read I would stare at it for a few minutes and then hand it back to them and ask them, "Well, what do you think?"

All through school and even initially on the job I wanted to be invisible. My self-esteem was so low that if I passed someone in the hall I would not look up and say hello unless they spoke first. I wanted to float through life invisible and unnoticed.

Looking back I am reminded of a quote by Les Brown.

Many people want to tiptoe through
life to get safely to death.
Les Brown

First Jobs

My first real job was trimming Christmas trees. My brother worked there and although you were supposed to be fourteen they let me in at thirteen. I was very small so I had to climb up the trees to trim them. The owners could see that I was trying very hard. I'm sure they kept me on because of my determination. I wrecked a few trees, but eventually I caught on.

When I was seventeen I was on a work program at school with the City of Perham, my hometown. I was in the Street Dept. We swept gutters, mowed lawns, maintained parks and things of that nature. I was promised a job when I graduated. I have always had a good attitude and a willingness to work hard. I still have this attitude today. I am not afraid to get my hands dirty or to get in there with anyone and do what has to be done. At seventeen I was all set to go to work in the Street Department of Perham.

My old uniform

When I graduated from high school, (sort of), a friend who was working at the Barrel Of Fun Potato Chip factory in Perham, Minnesota, convinced his managers that I was a hard worker and very good with my hands. I was offered a job at the factory and I took it because the pay was a better than working for the city. The Barrel of Fun Potato Chip factory was the big employer in Perham; back then they employed several hundred people and often worked three shifts.

I started as a machine operator because they knew I was mechanically inclined. I loved working with my hands building things and when I saw the Maintenance Department I said, "That's what I want to do." I expressed an interest in maintenance by working after hours with the maintenance crew, just helping out, on my own time, doing anything I could.

My old ofice

Eventually I was transferred into maintenance and within six months I was promoted to maintenance supervisor. This brought on a whole new set of challenges. Eventually I was transferred into maintenance and within six months I was promoted to maintenance supervisor. This brought on a whole new set of challenges. Soon all my co-workers in maintenance knew that I could not spell. Now I had to make out work orders and make lists of things to do. I would make out notes essentially for myself but be very hands-on in working with my crew. The men that worked with me liked the fact that I was there, in the trenches with them. It was really because I couldn't put anything on paper that I had to go in and show them how it was done.

My old tools of the trade.

What, kind of things did you do in Maintenance?

I really loved my work. I did everything, from general maintenance, greasing equipment, keeping it running, changing chains and sprockets, to building conveyers and mezzanines. I designed and built a potato bin where they stored trailer loads, tons of potatoes. I designed a conveyer system that today, ten years later, is still in use. I was maintaining equipment, designing equipment and building equipment and through all of the process being very hands-on.

As maintenance supervisor I earned the trust of my superiors. They saw my ability to build things and they began to take my word for what I thought needed to be done. My self-esteem and self-confidence were beginning to grow. I still wanted to crawl behind a rock every time anything to do with reading came up. I still wanted to be the invisible man, but my confidence was growing in my ability to do the job.

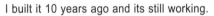

I built it 10 years ago and its still working.

I owe a great deal to the supervisors, managers and owners who I worked with at The Barrel of Fun. They showed confidence in me and had faith in my ability as a maintenance worker and as manager of the department.

This was it. I could not imagine a better job. I had arrived. John Haremza had it made.

And then I was introduced to network marketing and I began to dream

THE FACTORY TOUR

Most of us are so used to seeing John in a suit doing an opportunity meeting, a training meeting, on stage at a convention or on a video that we just cannot imagine him as a maintenance manager. As part of the process of writing this book John arranged a tour of the potato chip factory where he worked.

It was an interesting tour both from seeing where John worked and how he related to many of his old friends who were still on the job. The overwhelming impression as we walked out on the factory floor was that this was a large, hot, noisy and busy place. The uniform was shorts, hairnets and baseball caps. The talk was of hunting, fishing, boats and motors. The signs were typical factory signs, "Safety protects people, quality protects jobs". There was a safety bingo program that gave the lucky winner $150 if the plant achieved its safety objectives.

It was interesting to note John's pride in the things he built when he was maintenance manager; they ranged from small conveyors to a huge bin where potatoes were loaded from the trucks. You could have put a small house in this bin.

Several of John's old buddies were still working and to hear John talk to them about the various pieces of equipment they maintained it was as if he had never left. It was obvious that John had loved his job.

There were some interesting contrasts between the potato chip factory and John's life style today. It turns out that John missed out on some of the perks that came with his job. If he had only hung in for ten years he would have received a watch. Even more serious if he had hung in there for fifteen years he would have received two nights free at the Radison motel in Fargo. He also missed working 12 hour days and being called in at midnight and weekends to fix a piece of equipment that was holding up the line.

As we left John said, "You know it would have been easy to stay here, I liked the job, I had some real good friends, the company was good to me, management treated us well, the pay was good and I was in a comfort zone. I'm obviously glad I made the move but looking back I can see how it is often hard for a anyone to even imagine a life style like ours".

I must admit until I saw with my own eyes where John worked, the equipment he maintained, the office he used and the now famous break room, that I too had difficulty seeing John as a maintenance manager. But it's true, he did wear dark blue work clothes, his hands were covered with grease, he wore a hair net on the job, he was good at what he did, welding and fixing, and he took a great deal of pride in his profession. When I saw the break room I could imagine his co-workers telling him that he was crazy to leave his safe and secure job and that he would fail in this network-marketing scheme. I could hear John saying, "Well the worst that can happen is that I have to come back and get a job like yours".

It doesn't look like he will be going back there any time soon.

"You know it would have been easy to stay here".
John Haremza

Twenty years from now you will be more disappointed by the things you didn't do than by the things you did. So throw off the bowlines, sail away from the safe harbor. Catch the trade winds in your sails.
Explore. Dream.

Mark Twain

CHAPTER 3

Back to the
Starting Line

John you were doing well at NSA why did you leave?

My four years at NSA were an excellent learning experience and
I was starting to earn more money than I had ever earned in my life.
The first indication that there was a problem was when Jeff Olson, a
major player left. For the first time I took my blinders off and looked
around. I realized I had not heard of one new person who had made any
money since I joined the business. They were still telling the same
stories that I was told when I first got started. Jeff made a strong case
of the need for consumable products and the importance of timing.

The problem was we were dealing with non-consumable products.
You had to find new people every month to buy the product. There was
no leverage from a product perspective. I also learned an important
lesson about timing. By the time I really understood the business the

company was on the tail end of a massive momentum cycle with no new products and there I was, I had arrived, I was earning $5,000 a month, more money than I had ever made in my life.

The problems with NSA were serious, non-consumable products and the timing was wrong. The opportunity was perceived to be at a saturation point. You see it's not a matter of saturation, it's really a matter of perception. Everybody had heard of it. The whole business was driven off recruiting because there was no consumption, no ongoing product purchases to support residual income and no new products.

I was golfing one day with my best friend and fellow NSA distributor, Doug Overvold, I can still remember that Doug was uneasy. We were putting on the first green and Doug said, "John, there's no question, we're both going to make millions in network marketing, I just don't think it's going to be with this company." I had already come to the realization that we had a serious problem, but how could I hold my people? I had lost my belief in the company. What do I do, this is my livelihood? I was not willing to throw in the towel. I asked Doug, "Tell me what you're thinking." I knew what he was thinking; he and I thought a lot alike. He said, "I think that we need to find another company."

We began to research network marketing and together we looked at thirty different companies. We saw everything from multilevel dog food to BBQ sauce to condoms. Within the thirty companies we looked at, we found Rexall Showcase International.

How did you check out Rexall Showcase International? What were you were looking for? What did you like about the company?

This was going to be a serious decision. Cliff Overvold, Doug's father had joined us earlier and he had just reached the top position with NSA. Now, here we are, Doug and I telling him that we want to do something different. He felt like he just arrived, he was having fun and as far as he was concerned this was the deal. We had to tell him that this was not the deal and that we were going to look for something else. Initially, he was shocked. We began to do our research, looking at other companies.

One of the companies we looked at was Rexall Showcase International, a stable, very conservative company. It did not have the excitement, the flair that other companies had, but something about it grew on us. I'm not sure if it was the Rexall name, the products, the management team, the timing, the facilities or the caliber of distributor we saw in Todd Smith and Randy Schroeder.

We flew to Boca Raton to tour the facilities. One of the things that impressed us was the corporate facility. Take a tour of our facilities at your earliest possible opportunity. Damon DeSantis, now the President of Rexall Sundown, was then vice president of Rexall Showcase International. He picked the three of us up at the airport in his Q45, chauffeured us around Boca Raton, toured the facilities with us and took us to lunch. Todd Smith, our would-be sponsor, and Randy Schroeder, flew in to meet us in Boca Raton.

Ultimately it was Rexall Showcase International that got us excited and we decided to get on board and take this one "to the top".

My wife knew there was a problem, but I didn't tell her how concerned I was because we were making very good money. When I came home one day and said, "Honey, we're going to do something different." she thought I had gone off the deep end - again.

Cliff, Doug and I knew what we were looking for. We looked at five aspects of every opportunity, the company, the products, the compensation plan, the training, the support and the timing. Today I tell people that these are the five things to consider when they are looking at the right opportunity for them.

First the company: The one thing Rexall Showcase International had above every other company was a name that opens doors.   The biggest challenge we face is the image of network marketing. Rexall opens doors that would normally remain shut. It is a major asset in overcoming the network marketing stigma.

The products: I liked them because they were affordable, highly consumable and they addressed huge market concerns. The products were not gimmicky, not fads, they were main line, understandable products - and they worked.

The compensation plan: I could see how the combination of consumable products and a compensation plan that paid up to 10% on the 6th level would build and multiply the incomes of both full time and part time distributors.

The training and support: The training and support were unlike anything I had ever seen or experienced. It set the foundations for the excellent support we receive as distributors today.

The timing: The timing was not ideal. There were only a few products. Bios Life Diet 1 gave you gas and diarrhea, no one was making any serious money, but we were impressed by the facilities, the DeSantis family and the leadership of Randy, Todd, and Stewart. We could see that preventative health was the place to be.

Todd Smith sponsored us, Doug, Cliff and myself – all three of us started together. We drew straws to decide who would sponsor whom. I didn't draw the longest straw, but I didn't get the shortest one either. Todd sponsored Cliff, Cliff sponsored me and I sponsored Doug.

We came into Rexall with a different mind-set. We knew that network marketing worked because we had experienced some success in NSA. We were willing to invest. When I got started with NSA, I was not willing to invest. It was a case of a nickel holding up a dollar. I think that's what happens when some people come into the business. They are not willing to stake their life on it. It's that do-or-die attitude, where you're either going to do it or you're going to die, that leads to success. Burn your bridges behind you and don't look back. Most people leave a back door open just in case they decide to get out. We came into Rexall Showcase International without a back door. We put our life on the line and we went forward.

It's that do-or-die attitude, where you're either
going to do it or die, that leads to success.

The three of us were stacked and our goal was to drive Doug's organization deep. He was at the bottom and all three of us would generate revenue through his organization. In network marketing depth equals stability. It was a business strategy that worked for us.

The thing about duplication is that we all do exactly what our sponsor did for better or for worse. Todd introduced us to Rexall Showcase International through an ad in USAToday. We thought that this was the deal. We ran an ad in USAToday looking for people who had seen some success in network marketing thinking we would do the same thing with them that Todd had done with us. We were looking for people who understood the business, who could get off and running quickly. The problem is that the people who responded to our ad were looking at every company in the world. The other companies had a hype and excitement that we did not have back then. They looked better, they felt better, but logically, we had the best story. We did this for 90 days, running ads, spending a ton of money and seeing no success. We did not sponsor a single person.

We learned the hard way that your best market is your warm market, the people with whom you have some kind of association. Talk to the people you know, you will spend less money and see better results. Your warm market is your best bet.

A Sense of urgency: One of the keys to success in network marketing is to create a sense of urgency and a fear of loss. It was October when we began looking at Rexall Showcase International and

---

Burn your bridges behind you
and don't look back.

---

we were saying to ourselves "We're coming into Christmas, we're going to coast through NSA, get all our loose ends tied up, and we'll hit this thing hard the first of the year. Cliff had just purchased $50,000 worth of product to get to his position. I was making more money than I had ever made and I wanted to milk it a little longer. Randy put such of a fear of loss in us that we had to start today, right now or forget it. He created such a sense of urgency that we kicked off our business in November. We have never regretted that decision.

From faith to belief: When you join Rexall Showcase International you enter the business on faith. You may be very serious but at this point in your career you operate on faith. Faith turns to belief through participation in the business, meetings, three-way calls and particularly through major events such as corporate conferences. One of those key events is to tour our corporate facilities. You come out of that tour with a different attitude, a different posture. It will make a world of difference in your business as it did in mine.

The picture was crystal clear for us. We knew that everybody we were working with was going to sign up. I was sure that all of my people would join me.

I don't think I ever had more than 15 or 20 people in NSA at any given time because the attrition rate was so high and the company had no ongoing product consumption. Only two people came with me. One was my brother, who still has a distributorship and was quite active for a couple of years but ultimately he did not follow through. I believe that he will be back.

I had my brother and Kim Hegg, one of the first people I sponsored in NSA. Kim is a great guy but he just couldn't dig down deep inside himself to build enthusiasm and excitement. As for the rest of my people, one of two things happened, they either lost belief in network marketing and left the industry altogether or they were so upset with us leaving that they stayed and rode NSA to the bottom.

Other than exchanging Christmas cards Kim and I had lost touch. I called him just this summer. We went fishing and talked about old times, he has gone back to his old profession in car sales. "Come on back Kim the timing is better than it has ever been".

I built Rexall with non-networkers, with a whole new group of people. I came from NSA with experience on what to do, how to do it and with a strong belief in network marketing. I was willing to invest, not to do what I did before and have a nickel hold up a dollar. I came into Rexall Showcase International focused, with a clear direction in mind. I experienced my share of disappointments, particularly knowing that everybody from NSA was going to join me and they didn't. I had just reached a point in NSA where I was making money, my credit cards were paid off and we were living well. I had to start the whole process all over again. I went massively back into debt. My wife was sure I was going to put us in the poor house and the rest of my family and her family knew that I was nuts. I kept my blinders on, I kept going forward, I stayed focused and the rest is history.

The opportunity before us in Rexall Showcase International today is much greater than when Cliff, Doug and I got started. We have

> *When a thing is done, it's done. Don't look*
> *back. Look forward to your next objective.*
> George C. Marshall

the right tools in place, we have an outstanding product line that gets stronger at every conference, we have a very impressive management team, we have the most sophisticated and professional distributor force in the world and we are in many more countries. We're small enough as a company that you can get as much of this as you want. We have 80% of our growth in front of us and that is just to our first billion. Do you really think that we will stop there? We're big enough as a company to have a track record of success, the management team, the facilities and the finances to take us to the next level.

The vision and the possibilities are so much clearer today than they were five years ago or even three years ago. I am convinced that this is the time and this is the place and Rexall Showcase International is the opportunity that will take us "to the top".

John we often hear success stories of individuals making huge incomes within a few months of getting started. Is this typical of the industry? What did you earn your first few years in the business?

It is possible to earn a great deal of money very quickly in this business; however, I believe that my income over the past 9 years is typical for most distributors. Remember that I was doing the business full time within six months of getting started with NSA.

My first year with NSA I earned $18,000, my second year $26,000, $50,000 my third year and $102,000 my fourth year.

My first year with Rexall I earned $76,000, my second year $189,000, and I earned $346,000 my third year. After my third year, I took some time off, bought a lake home, began re-modelling and moved to San Diego for the winter. There were a lot of distractions that year and my business began to slip. My fourth year, my income dropped to $306,000. If you're careful you can get by on that but I did not like the feeling of going backward.   I got active in my fifth year and built my income back up to $326,000. It went to $416,000 this year (1999) and I can see it going well over half a million in the near term.

When I took a lot of time off in my fourth year it slowed me down and it took almost two years to get back in the trenches and to recover my momentum. I was comfortable and comfortable is nice for awhile, but what makes us feel alive, what makes our blood pump, is growing as a person.   I wanted to grow again, to go to the next level; there was no satisfaction in standing still. I know now that I am a happier person when I am in active pursuit of my goals.

NSA			Rexall Showcase	
year one	$	18,000	year one	$ 76,000
year two	$	26,000	year two	$189,000
year three	$	50,000	year three	$346,000
year four	$	102,000	year four	$306,000
year five	$	326,000		
year six	$	416,000		

PLEASE NOTE:

There are no guarantees expressed or implied by these earnings. Different individuals will experience different results based on their experience, the skills they bring to this business, their level of desire and on how hard they work. These earnings are not meant as guarantees.

Everyone thinks of changing the world, but no one thinks of changing himself.

Leo Tolstoy

If it's to be ... it's up to me.

Anonymous

The poor man is not he who is without a cent, but he who is without a dream.

Harry Kemp

Trust your hopes, not your fears.

David Mahoney

Milestones on the Journey to Success

What are the elements of success in Rexall Showcase International?

How can you make your dream your reality?

What are the milestones to look for on your way "to the top"?

For you to say, "I'm going to the top" and have it ring true, what will you have to do?

"Success is not an accident, success leaves clues."
Anthony Robbins

"Become all that you were created capable of being,
expand your full growth and show yourself at
length in your own shape and stature."

Thomas Carlyle must have had tremendous respect
for your potential when he wrote those words.

Bob Proctor

CHAPTER 4

Personal Growth

John, one of the things that you talk about all the time is personal development. You say that what you become in this business is far more important than the money you make.

There is no question in my mind that personal growth is the key to success in our business. As Jim Rohn says, "Work harder on yourself than you do at your job. When you work at your job, you make a living, when you work on yourself, you'll make a fortune."

Network marketing is pretty simple. A big part of the business is that people buy people. You need to become buyable. I believe that my commitment to ongoing personal growth is responsible for 80% of the success I've enjoyed. Obviously you must have the commitment and the burning desire to follow your personal growth with action, doing the right things to build your business.

When people ask me, "John, what are the things that make the most difference?" my first response is always "personal growth", a commitment to become more, so that you can do more and have more. I usually quote some of my favorite tape programs. Napoleon Hill in his book "Think and Grow Rich" emphasizes fundamentals that do not change regardless of the business or profession.

My all time favorite tape sets are "Lead the Field and The Strangest Secret" by Earl Nightingale. Jim Rohn's "The Art of Exceptional Living" is, well exceptional. I like Lou Tice in "Mastering the Attitude of Achievement."

Zig Ziglar has always been one of my favorites. Zig says that you must "BE" before you can "DO" and you must "DO" before you can "HAVE". Your focus must be on becoming the leader you must become to be successful in network marketing. These speakers talk a lot about fundamentals, principles and philosophies. They talk about reshaping your life one step at a time by changing your philosophies. Jim Rohn talks about being 25, behind on his rent, behind on his payments, behind on his promises and broke. His mentor asked, "Why are you continuing to do what's not working? Who sold you on that philosophy?"

Make a commitment to BE more, so that you
can DO more and HAVE more.

Zig Ziglar

Could you give us an example of personal development in your life?

The best example is my journey from one extreme to another. What better illustration of personal growth is there than my journey from school, trying to be invisible, afraid of my own shadow, to going to work as a maintenance manager, building some self-confidence, to networking marketing being treated as an equal and ultimately to a standing ovation from 8,000 professionals in Orlando? Tell me that personal growth is not important! Tell me that you do not grow as a person in this business!

The first thing that blew me away at Rexall Showcase International was being treated as an equal by a successful person like Todd Smith. Todd was making more in a month than I used to make in a year and here he was treating me like an equal, like a real person. This was much different than the company environment I was accustomed to.

Ultimately I was treated like a celebrity. It is a great feeling, but it is a bit uncomfortable. You know that underneath you're just like everyone else. It's strange to have people come up and say how they love you, love your tapes, love your materials, love your story and even wanting your autograph. At our conference in Orlando I told my own personal story for the first time in a long time. For me it brought back painful memories but I know that telling my story of overcoming challenges, of climbing mountains, of "going to the top" empowers others. I could not make it through the lobby without being thanked by many, many people. I wanted to take time with each one of them, with everybody who wanted to talk to me, not just to make them feel important, but to let them know that they are important.

Most of us lack the self-discipline to do every day, day after day, the things we need to do. Anthony Robbins has a set of tapes on 30 days to total power. You listen to a tape every day and take some specific action. On tape two he says, "Congratulations, you have just made it further than 80% of the people who bought this tape set". Isn't that something? People make the investment in excellent material and 80% of them never get to the second tape.

We see this all the time when we're prospecting. People who are miserable in their lives and yet continue to do the same things over and over again, not willing to take the steps that will change their lives.

When I think back to my days at the Barrel of Fun Potato Chip factory, I was talking to people all around me about this business, I was on fire. Which one of them saw it? How many took action? Everyone teased me and told me I was crazy, yet every day they continued to complain about their jobs. They knew that they were going nowhere but they were unwilling to make any changes.

Once you have been given an alternative, when an opportunity has been put in front of you and you decide to pass, I believe that you lose the right to complain. You have made a conscious, deliberate decision to stay where you are. In essence you have said "My mind is made up, don't confuse me with the facts.

I don't like it here, I don't like what I'm doing, I don't like what I'm earning, I don't like what I have become .. BUT .. I am not going to change, I am going to stay here."

---

*The classic definition of insanity is to keep on
doing the same things you have always done
and expect to see different results.*

Who would you drive 100 miles to listen to?

I would drive 100 miles to listen to a lot of people. I think that we all need to be students of anyone that has been successful, they all have something to offer. You're not going to accept everything; you're not going to agree with everything you hear. Take the best and leave the rest.

I would drive 100 miles to listen to the people I've mentioned – Jim Rohn, Zig Ziglar, Brian Tracy, Anthony Robbins. I'd drive 100 miles to listen to Todd Smith, Randy Schroeder, Stewart Hughes or to any of the leaders in Rexall Showcase International. You can learn so much from the leaders in our business. It is not always new knowledge; it may be a reminder of some of the basics we all forget.

People come into this business and say, "I've seen all that stuff. I've listened to all that stuff". One thing I've learned is that people who are full of themselves or people "who know it all" will not make it in our business.

When there's somebody you can learn from and become a better person, a better leader, be there.

I have learned that when everything is said and done there is usually a lot more said than done.

What individuals have been the most influential people in your life?

From a motivational perspective, I would have to say Earl Nightingale, Zig Ziglar and Jim Rohn. They taught me more about life, the philosophy of success and the philosophy of life than anyone else.

From a leader and network marketing perspective, for someone who lives their life with integrity and is the kind of person I strive to be it's Todd Smith. Todd has made a positive difference in the lives of literally thousands of us. Randy Schroeder has been an invaluable source of knowledge and motivation. Stewart Hughes has set a standard of excellence that I constantly strive to attain.

If you think you can win, you can win.

Faith is necessary to victory.
William Hazlitt

Whether you think you can or you think you can't, you're right.
Henry Ford

All the resources we need are in the mind.
Theodore Roosevelt

CHAPTER 5

Elements of Success

John, looking back over your years in the business, what would you say are the elements of success in network marketing?

There are many elements to success in this business.

Enthusiasm: Enthusiasm is a major key to success. The old saying is, "If you set yourself on fire people will travel for miles to watch you burn." When I got started in this business I was on fire, I didn't know what I was talking about and when I was done, the people didn't know what I was talking about, but they still wanted to do the business. They said, "We don't know what you're doing, but we want to do it, too."

Set yourself on fire and people will travel for miles to watch you burn.

Relationships: The element that I would put at the top of the list is understanding that this is a relationship business. People buy people. Essentially we are dealing with a volunteer army. It's not so much what you say; it's how you feel about what you say that really counts. Fake, put-on-a-show, insecure people will not make it in this business long-term. You must build long-lasting relationships based on trust, integrity and character.

The Pipeline Principle: Many people come into this business and they immediately focus their energy on one, two or three people. The odds that these people will say 'no' are very high. Think of your prospect base, your warm market as a pipeline. The "pipeline principle" is that you're filling your pipeline and you do not have time to talk to those who aren't interested. This creates a sense of urgency and a fear of loss.

"If you're not ready right now, that's fine because I've got many other people to talk to."

That's enthusiasm, it creates a fear of loss. Keep your pipeline so full of prospects - listening to tapes, watching videos, coming to meetings, participating in three way calls and you will never wonder who you should talk to next.

Pay the price: Every profession, every business demands that you pay the price. Behind every successful person, there's a story. Whether with Rexall Showcase or at some other time in their life, they have paid the price. This business will pay you exactly what you're worth. You need to become worth more; you must build yourself.

Never give up, never, never, never, never give up.

It is unfortunate that so many people enter a business like this and think they're going to be rich overnight. It takes time to make it work. People try this business for six months and they don't think it's working because they're not making the money they expected to make. They drop out of the business and go back to their regular job where they have been for years.

Their job did not and will not make them rich in 40 years. Most jobs do not have the potential to make anyone rich - not in a million years.

Give yourself time to grow: Hold the vision. Stay the course. Stay on target. Pay the price.

Recruit up: This is a significant principle for success in Rexall Showcase International. I tell people, "Wherever you are, picture yourself on a scale of 1 to 10 and put yourself at 5. No matter how successful you have been, rank yourself as a 5.

Now go out and talk to 5's and above. We all face the temptation to recruit people who really need the business, those who have not been as successful as we have. We do not feel uneasy when we approach them.

What happens if you start the trend this way? You talk to 4's, the 4's talk to 3's, the 3's talk to the 2's and before you know it you've got a group of couch potatoes. Always recruit up. The most successful distributors are those who recognize this principle.

Pay the price.   Hold the vision.
Stay the course.   Stay on target.

Please don't misunderstand me. I do not equate success with the pocketbook. I equate success with the person their integrity, their character, their work ethic, not with what they earn or what they own. The one thing I always look for in a person is desire; desire is the one thing you can not teach. You can't put the heart in a lion.

Follow the system: A successful franchise always follows a proven formula. Rexall Showcase International has an excellent system. It works. If it worked for Todd Smith, Randy Schroeder, Stewart Hughes and for me, will it work for you? Follow the system. Humble yourself; accept the fact that you don't know it all. This is not to say you can't come up with new ideas, they are always welcome, but until you become successful, follow the system.

Use your upline: You're not alone in this business. Understand that you're in business for yourself but not by yourself. You have an entire upline of people who know that your success is as important to them as their success. Your success is what guarantees their ongoing success. Use your upline, they have more experience than you do. They have made all the mistakes so that you don't have to make them. They have a track record of success and they are free, their support will not cost you a penny. Your best friend in the business should be your immediate upline.

My sponsor, my immediate upline is not following the system. He is not attentive; in fact he pays absolutely no attention to me. What should I do?

If your sponsor is not working with you to build your business then go upline until you find someone who will work with you. It is your responsibility to find and utilize the resources you need to be successful in this business. The Rexall Showcase International corporate philosophy is reflected in our compensation plan - it motivates leaders to support anyone in their organization who is willing to ask for help and to follow through on the help they receive. I would not be where I am today if it had not been for the support I received from Todd Smith, Randy Schroeder and Stewart Hughes.

Focus on one opportunity at a time: The second you sign up with Rexall Showcase International some mysterious force broadcasts that you are in the business and you are suddenly besieged with other network marketing opportunities. Many of them will be slick money games and their pitch is that you can do their deal in addition to Rexall Showcase International. They will tell you that their deal is complimentary to yours and will actually help you build your Rexall business. Don't believe them. Do not fall into the trap. The instant you take your eye off the ball you lose momentum. If you present another opportunity to your downline, you will lose them from Rexall Showcase International and you will not have the credibility to bring them into your new deal. Stay focused. Many of the failures people experience in this business are because they get distracted with other ventures or other things going on in their life. It's extremely important to maintain a focus. Put your blinders on and go straight ahead.

When you are approached take a positive, proactive stance. **"I'm not interested in your deal but you need to take a look at Rexall Showcase International."** If you agree to look at theirs if they look at yours, this is what will happen. You will be thinking of how to destroy their deal and present yours all the time they are talking. They of course will be thinking the same way when you present your deal.

Be patient with your prospects: How long did it take you to make the decision to get on board with Rexall Showcase International? Most of us spent a few days, a few weeks, even a few months thinking about the business. Yet here we go, every time we talk to someone, we expect him or her to see it now and come in as a Director. Give people time to think about it, to absorb the information. I'm still not sure how to balance patience with creating a sense of urgency ... if you have the answer let me know.

Be patient with your distributors: Regardless of their background, your new distributors will go through a steep 6 to 12 month learning curve as they learn the subtleties of network marketing and the strengths of Rexall Showcase International. Give them time, be patient. You may have to explain the same thing several times to a new distributor. You may have to coach them every day. They are, in the final analysis, your keys to success. If they do well, you will do well. Don't despair, you learned the business the same way that they must learn the business.

Be patient with yourself: We live in a society that demands instant gratification, we want it now, right now. This business does not work like that. It is not a get-rich-quick scheme. You will not become a leader overnight. Be patient with yourself, listen to Rexall tapes, watch the videos, work with your upline, be at every meeting, be on the conference calls, attend every convention and follow the system. Maintain a sense of urgency but at the same time be patient with yourself.

This is a business of plateaus, it can be an emotional roller coaster: When people ask me, "John, what's the catch with this opportunity?", I tell them the catch is that this business is an emotional roller coaster. You will have unbelievable highs and unbelievable lows often the same day and sometimes within the same hour. You will have a prospect planning to come in as a Director and suddenly they don't return your calls ... move on. You will have a new distributor who has all the skills to set the world on fire and then he refuses to follow the system. Within a few weeks he is out of the business ... move on.

The most important word in this business may well be "NEXT". It's not a matter of if you're going to get knocked down; you will get knocked down. The question is are you going to get back up?

Remember this:

SW - SW - SW - SW - N

Some will - some won't - so what

- some waiting - Next!

Be responsible: To be responsible and to take responsibility are part of becoming a leader. Many times, due to immaturity, we find that distributors are not ready or not willing to take responsibility. When a new distributor asks how they can solve a problem instead of asking their upline to do it for them, you have a potential leader.

Be the leader: The speed of the pack is the speed of the leader. You are a role model, a mirror – often, a merciless mirror of your downline. People will pick up your bad habits as well as your good habits. Be the leader you would like your upline to be. To become a leader you must make a conscious, deliberate, definite decision to the growth process, the learning and the doing that will make you a leader.

Its easier to give birth than to raise the dead: One of the lessons I have learned over the past 9 years is that it is easier to give birth than to raise the dead. It is easier to go out and find a new distributor than it is to work with a distributor who does not want to work hard, to follow the system and to be coachable. This is certainly one of the big keys in our business; by far the biggest mistake that distributors make is that they spend time with the wrong people. You can waste an entire year with the wrong person. Match energy with energy. When a new distributor is sending out tapes and following the system, extend yourself and work with them. If a distributor is not returning phone calls and not working the system, move on - remember the magic word - NEXT. We want everyone to do well, but we can't sacrifice ourselves in the process. I'm not talking about forgetting anybody, we want everybody to be successful, but you can't push a rope.

Develop an owner attitude: Someone once told me that attitude is everything. My response was "I don't know if attitude is everything. I believe that attitude is the only thing."

We must develop an owner attitude Vs an employee attitude. Many people come into this business with a job mentality, a job attitude, and a day's work for a day's pay. Things don't work like that in network marketing, you may work for a month with no reward in fact there are cases in Rexall Showcase International where distributors worked very hard and followed the system for months with no payback. Develop an owner attitude. This is your business. You are building your own long-term success.

Randy Schroeder says it best on his tape Recruit the Only Way to Success, "This business is the closest thing you will ever get to a guarantee of success, if you just keep working the plan, getting tapes out and following up, you will be successful. The recruiting game is a numbers game and you have to play the game."

It's easy to, it's easy not to: Jim Rohn says that there are always a few simple things that make the most difference, that lead to success. These are simple things; they are easy to do. The problem is that they are easy not to do. One of the problems with our business is that it is so easy to get in. For $49.50 you can buy a distributor kit and now you're in business with all the resources of Rexall Showcase International behind you. The problem is that it is just as easy to get out, to quit. When the extent of your investment is $49.50 you have not made a serious commitment to your long-term success. This same principle applies to all the simple things we need to do to build long term success.

Attitude is the only thing.

It's Easy To ......It's Easy Not To

It's easy to put your goals in writing.	It's easy not to.
It's easy to write your warm list of 100 names	It's easy not to.
It's easy to drop a tape in the mail	It's easy not to.
It's easy to make a follow up call	It's easy not to.
It's easy to do a three-way call.	It's easy not to.
It's easy to ask your sponsor for help.	It's easy not to.
It's easy to get to the weekly meeting.	It's easy not to.
It's easy to get to the corporate conferences.	It's easy not to.
It's easy to monitor your own progress.	It's easy not to.

Do the "**easy to's**" and they will take you to the top.

Do the "**easy not to's**" and they will take you nowhere. For the rest of your life you can be one of those "woulda, coulda, shoulda, if-only-I'd-a, I-knew-it-when" people.

Jim Rohn on attitude:

You say, "It's easy to have a great attitude, just look at her success." I say this, "Maybe the success is there because of her attitude."

Good news goes down bad news goes up: If you are face-to-face with a problem discuss it with your upline not your downline. In our business good news always goes down to everyone in your organization. If there is a problem share it with your upline. If possible solve the problem yourself, take responsibility. If you cannot resolve it on your own take it to your upline.

Distractions: In our business distractions are inevitable, they are part of the journey. In some cases the distractions are in our minds. Doug, Cliff and I got started in November seven years ago. December was our first month and we built the business right through Christmas. It was a phenomenal month. We had no real comprehension of the products or the business back then but we just went out and did it. People who are serious don't care what time of year it is or what time of day it is, they want to talk to you now, right now. They bring a sense of urgency to the business. Many times we let both real and imagined distractions divert us from the business.

The 90-day plan: One of the nice things about this business is that you can always start over. You can make the next 90 days the turning point in your life and in your business. This is the time right now to get yourself fired up, to move forward, and to pick up market share. Commit yourself to a 90-day run to get your business off the ground, to get your business heading in the right direction. Doug Overvold's 90-day plan is an excellent way to start your business all over again, big time.

People who are serious don't care what time of year it is or what time of day it is, they want to talk to you now, right now.

Be the sponsor you would sign up with: The other thing that I feel very passionate about is the need to step back, take a look in the mirror and analyze how you're approaching this business. Dan Swindell said something at a corporate conference that sticks in my mind. He sat back one day and took a real good look at how he was approaching the business, particularly how he was talking to other people. He asked himself, "If I were trying to sponsor me, could I do it?" He had to be honest with himself and the answer was, "I don't think so, I don't think I could sponsor me." It all comes back to the fact that people buy people. It's not so much what you say; it's how you feel about what you say. It's the passion, the enthusiasm, and the belief that comes from within that brings people into your organization. The person who has the greatest belief will always win, will always attract others to the business. We're selling hope. We're selling opportunity. We have the answers. We have the best opportunity in the world and we are sharing it with anyone who will listen. Our attitude must be "If you don't see it, I must have missed something in sharing it with you".

Take time tonight to look at your business, what is your attitude, how do you talk to people, what are you doing, what could you do better? Look in the mirror and ask yourself, "Could I sponsor me right now? Am I as good as my sponsor? Am I as good as the sponsor I wish I had?"

A leader sells hope, dreams and opportunity.
A leader is a dealer in hope.

WHEN I LOOK IN THE MIRROR WHAT DO I SEE?

I am committed to personal growth.   _____

My goals are in writing.   _____

I reviewed my goals in the last 30 days.   _____

I know my downline leader's "WHY's".   _____

I have reviewed my leader's goals with them   _____

I am always ready to help my people.   _____

My people look to me for leadership.   _____

There were more people at my weekly meeting
    this week than last week.   _____

Do I set a good example for my people?   _____

Am I the best recruiter in my organization?   _____

Am I the best trainer in my organization?   _____

What is my attitude to the business?   _____

When was the last time I spoke to my leaders?   _____

When did I speak to my weakest distributor?   _____

I listened to Todd's training tapes.   Date   _____

Could I sponsor me?   _____

Would I sponsor me?   _____

If I signed up under me, would I get the support I
    need to see my dreams become my reality?   _____

Do I like the person in the mirror?   _____

New Products: As we write this book our new Ultimate Perform-ance product line has just been introduced. The home team has made a commitment to introduce at least one new product at every national con-vention, twice a year. How do we integrate new products into our business?

There are two approaches we can take. One group of distributors will run out to the health clubs and fitness centers and start talking to muscle-bound, body-builders. They will find that these people know a whole lot more about these products than we do. This will be a frustrating exper-ience. My experience is that these are not the people who will build a business. We always have superior products and you will sell some product, but is that your goal? In my opinion, the Ultimate Performance products give us another reason to talk to a new group of people, to share with them the opportunity that we have with Rexall in making more money, building freedom, building a business. This has been the consensus of opinion on the Presidential Board of Advisors and throughout the leadership.

I believe that this is true with all of our new product announce-ments. We are selling a broad-brush approach; we're addressing huge concerns in the marketplace. New products are there to open the door, to create an interest.

What is our true product? What are we selling? We're selling opportunity. We're selling hope. We're giving people a new chance. That is and it must be our focus. If we don't take that focus, we will sell some products, but we will not capture the momentum that our company is experiencing and will continue to experience.

Every new product announcement gives us a reason to go back and contact people we have talked to in the past.

When will my organization take on a momentum of its own? When will it become a self-supporting business?

This is a common question. We all work very hard to get started, to get our organization together and working. When does an organization take on a life of its own? When does it become a self-sufficient, self-maintaining business?

Imagine that you're pushing a boulder up a hill. You have to keep your eye on the boulder, maintain your focus, maintain your energy level, and keep your commitment to roll that boulder to the top of the hill. This is the equivalent of making the Century Club. In our business when you have done $100,000 in product sales a month for two months in a row with $20,000 from a second leg, you have made the Century Club. Now you have enough people making enough money to keep this thing going, whether you work it or not. This $100,000 plateau is where security starts, where your organization will take on a momentum of its own.

Take a breather at this point and then continue to push even harder until you get to $200,000 a month. At $200,000 a month in total organizational pay-line volume your organization is unstoppable. Now your organization is a self-sustaining, self-sufficient business.

Of course by this time you are having so much fun working with your front line directors, spending the money and attending Century Club events that you do not want to stop working. Now your greatest thrill comes when you see your people seeing their dreams become their realities.

Now you know the secret:

Focus your first 90 days or your next 90 days
on getting your business off the ground.

Drive your business to $100,000 a month
and join the Century Club.

Take a breather and then continue
pushing until you get
to $200,000.

Now you have it made. How do you
like the view from the top?

Tough times don't last, tough people do.
Dr. Schulyer

Life is like a grindstone. Whether it grinds us down or polishes us up depends on us.
L. Thomas Holdcroft

The difference between a successful person and others is not a lack of knowledge, but rather a lack of will.
Vince Lombardi

CHAPTER 6

Sacrifices Along
the Way

John, one of the things we seldom talk about is the sacrifice involved in building long-term success in network marketing. What did you have to sacrifice to build the success you have attained?

When I heard about network marketing, I began to dream, but my dreams were small. I thought, if I could make $3,000 a month and be in business for myself, I would be out of my mind. I wouldn't know what to do with the money. Once I reached $3,000, I thought wouldn't $5,000 be nice? That would really take the edge off. Once I got to $5,000 I started looking for $10,000 a month and the business just took off on its own. Along the way, when I was a part-time distributor, trying to make the business work, I had to make sacrifices.

There is no question that our business requires sacrifices. This is one of the areas in which our industry has earned a bad name. You have people and sometimes companies selling their opportunity as an easy, no-money-down, no-sweat, get-rich-quick, once-in-a-lifetime opportunity.

"You're broke and homeless today? Don't worry, sign here, bring in three people and you'll be a millionaire tomorrow." This is a scam. There is no such thing as get-rich-quick, not if it's a legitimate long-term business.

If it looks too good to be true, it probably is.
Brian Tracy

It takes commitment, it takes perseverance, and it takes sacrifice. You pay the price now or you pay the price later. If you're going to be a success you will have to make some sacrifices, you may have to stop doing some of the things that you love to do.

When I got involved with Rexall Showcase International I had to give up some things. Before I got involved in network marketing one of three things would happen after work. We would head down to the local pub and have a few drinks. In winter and our winters were long, we used to go out to the fish house, do some ice fishing, have dinner and play cards. It was fun. I looked forward to it; to this day I still miss it. In summertime it was fishing and swimming at the lake; these were good times with my buddies. I gave it all up. It was not just the pain of what I was giving up, even worse was the harassment and kidding by my buddies. "Why aren't you with us? What are you doing? You're wasting your time."

By this time I had something that they did not have, something that they could not see. I had hope. I had a dream. I remember someone questioning me about my sacrifices, all the stuff I was missing. They seriously questioned what I was hoping to accomplish. In the end I said, "You know, the one thing I have, that you don't have, is a dream, a chance. You have no chance with what you're doing. At least I have a chance." Yes there were sacrifices but I was willing to make them. I had a dream and I was hungry.

As I look back on the conversations at the local pub and at the fish house they were all negative. My buddies would complain about the company, their job, their boss and their pay. I found it interesting after I got into network marketing, that even though they were given an opportunity to change their circumstances they did not want to change. I know that I gave them the opportunity to change as I was changing. They were comfortable in their complaining. I believe that once you have been given an opportunity to change, to better your life, you give up the right to complain if you say no.

It is hard to pay the price when the picture is not clear: I had a clear vision, an image of where I saw this going. I kept this vision in front of me just waiting for those few negative people who move around a lot. They did find me, believe me the dream stealers found me and they worked me over. You can be sure that they are going to find you, knock on your door, barge right in and work you over. You must have a clear vision of where you're going if you hope to defeat them. Keep your vision clear and right in front of you. Know what your, "end in mind" is.

You've got to be hungry.
Les Brown

The Emperor

There is a fable about an emperor who years ago gathered together the wisest sages in his kingdom and said, "I want you to assemble all the great knowledge of our civilization so that it is easily available for future generations." His sages worked for many years before returning with 10 large bound volumes. His highness glanced at the stack of books, frowned, and said, "Too long." The sages scurried from his throne room. They did not return until they had edited the ten volumes down to one large volume. However, when they handed it to the emperor, he refused to open it. "Still too lengthy," he said. Over the next two years, the sages condensed the book into one paragraph. The emperor was still not satisfied. Finally, these wise sages came back with a single sentence inscribed on a very small slip of paper. The emperor read it, smiled, and announced, "This is perfect. Now future generations will understand why we have been so successful. All the genius we possess is contained in this brilliant, solitary, phrase."

The phrase read: "There is no free lunch."

For most people the idea of sacrifice is foreign; it is difficult. They are not comfortable with it. If we could go back to my old workplace and lay out the opportunity, with my life today as an example, and give my buddies a guarantee that if they did what I did, they would have what I have, everyone of them would have to say, "I'm going to do it". The question is would they make the sacrifices that I made? I believe that if they had a clear picture, a vision of what their lives could be, they would follow me.

The picture must be clear but initially you must operate on faith. You have to operate on faith when the end of the month comes and your check is much smaller than you thought it was going to be. You have to hold the vision and stay the course.

Another saying from Earl Nightingale: "It's hard to throw wood in the fire when the heat is not there." When the heat's there, everybody will gather round and help stoke the fire. But it's tough to get it started, to go out and gather the wood when its cold and the heat is not there. That's what you have to do, there are no shortcuts. You must stay focused on the long-term picture.

A couple of examples I relate to our business. I heard a story once about a pianist who was marvellous – his fingers just danced across the keyboards, he would take people's breath away when he played. An admirer approached him after a concert and said, "I would do anything to play like you play." the pianist challenged him; he said, "No, you wouldn't.". He responded, "Yes I would. I would do anything to play the piano like you." Again the pianist responded, "No, you would not". After a few moments of uncomfortable silence, the pianist finally went on to explain, "Would you practice and practice and practice, staying up all hours of the night and beating on the keys until your fingers were bloody? That's what it takes."

The same thing applies to our business. People say, "John, I would do anything to make the kind of money you're making and to live your lifestyle." My immediate response is, "Great, that's what I need, you're the kind of person I've been looking for. Let's get started. We do meetings every Thursday night. You need to be there. How many people can you bring?" Now they say, "Did you say Thursday night? I bowl on Thursday night." This is the same person who if I told them Tuesday night would say, "Tuesday night, did you say Tuesday night? The Simpsons are on Tuesday night I can't make it." They are obviously not prepared to make the sacrifices that this business demands. As Todd Smith says, "You must discipline yourself to do the things you know you must do even when you don't feel like doing them." That's what will bring you success. When others are out playing, do the things you know you need to do. You may feel a little pain in the process but I can tell you this, it's worth it.

One sacrifice you must expect is the loss of some friends. If you are working this business and doing the things you must do, you will be growing. In most cases the people around you will not be growing. You will begin to see different visions and to live in different worlds. I enjoyed my time as a Maintenance Manager. I liked the people I worked with, they were and they still are good solid folks.

You must discipline yourself to do the things,
you know you should do, even when you don't
feel like doing them.

Todd Smith

We had fun together. When I decided to do the business, it was an unspoken message that what I had been doing with them was no longer good enough for me. It made them uncomfortable and those relationships began to fade. Even today when I go back, we can talk about old times, about fishing, hunting and the job but there is a barrier. I wish it were not so, but it is.

People are either going to join you or they're going to resist you. As a general rule people want you to do well, just not better. It is important to understand this aspect of our business.

Earl Nightingale talks about being a victim of our environment. We are a mirror of those we hang around with. If you want to grow as a person, if you want to be successful, you need to hang around with like-minded people. Spend your time with people with similar visions, goals and dreams.

I could still go out with the people I used to hang around with, have a drink with them and a few laughs but essentially our worlds are so different that we would have very little in common. If I needed something, I know that they would be there for me. I would certainly be there for them. Am I as close to them as I used to be? No, nowhere near.

Today I have friends in all 50 states and four countries. You could drop me from an aeroplane, hopefully with a parachute, and no matter where I landed someone there would take me in. It's not just the relationships; it's the quality of those relationships. It's knowing people who appreciate your contributions, who want to learn from you. The other side of the coin is that now I know that I can learn something from everybody I meet.

Looking back I gave up the pub, the fish house and hunting. These were not easy sacrifices but today I can fish anywhere in the world, the world is my fishing ground.

Were all my sacrifices worth it? You bet they were!

As a Maintenance Manager my world was within a 200-mile radius of Perham. Today I travel the world.

- A few months ago the Rexall Showcase International home team arranged for us to play softball with some future Hall of Famers. It was exciting.

- A few years ago Rexall Showcase International rented the Atlanta Astrodome and we played softball.

- I have been fishing on the Polar ice cap.

- Rexall Showcase International arranged for us to sail with the Olympic Sailing Team that competes in the America Cup.

- I've met Peter Fonda and had dinner with Roger Staubach.

---

*Measure the pain of failure against the pain of
getting out of your comfort zone.*
John Berta

This is my WHY, my dream.

_____

_____

These are the sacrifices I will make to
see my dream become my reality.

_____

_____

_____

_____

_____

_____

_____

_____

Are you going to lead or follow?
John Berta

If you want to be respected,
you must respect yourself.
Anonymous

Success is dependent on effort.
Sophocles

All life is an experiment.
The more experiments you make the better.
Ralph Waldo Emerson

CHAPTER 7

The Attributes
of a Leader

John, I hear a lot of talk about being a leader. What are the attributes of a leader? What makes a distributor a leader in Rexall Showcase International?

The first thing is to be an attractive person. As I say that, I don't mean physically, although I do believe it is important to look good, to be dressed properly, to be clean and well groomed. What I mean by being an attractive person is to be someone people want to be around. There are two types of people in this world, those who brighten a room when they come in and those who brighten a room when they leave. Be someone others want to be around.

The second item is follow-through. So many times as I was building my business, I made a commitment, I said was going to do something and then I failed to do it. Unfortunately I see this over and over and over again. I have made a commitment that I will not say I'm going to do something unless I know I can follow through. A leader is a person who follows through. When you follow through your people know they can count on you. They know that when you say something, you mean it, you're going to be there for them and they can count on you. If Todd Smith promises to call you at 9:15 on a Tuesday evening, I can guarantee you that at 9:15 Tuesday evening your phone will ring and Todd will be on the line.

Be the example: The speed of the pack is the speed of the leader. You must understand that people will pick up your bad habits as well as your good habits. This example applies in everything you do from your recruiting efforts to your commitment to personal growth to using the products and being a product of the product. Remember that you teach more by what you do than by what you say.

Care about your distributors: Care more about your distributors than you do about yourself. One of Zig Ziglar's all time, best known sayings is, "You can have everything you want in this world if you help enough other people get what they want." This will require short term sacrifices, but it will pay back big time over the long term.

Be a good listener: This is our most common failing. There is no doubt that a key attribute to leading is first being a good listener. You can't listen and you can't learn when you're talking. One of Stephen Covey's Seven Secrets of Highly Effective People is, "Seek first to understand, then to be understood." Listen 70% of the time. Be sure you understand where the speaker is coming from and how he or she

---

Listen 70% ------ Talk 30%

---

feels about their topic. Get behind the words to the feelings. Listening carefully shows a great deal of respect for the individual you're with. You have two ears and one mouth, use them accordingly.

Give honest feedback: To be a good coach you must give honest feedback. Todd Smith has been my coach in the business. Talk about someone who is willing to give honest feedback! Todd has always been straight and to the point. He is always direct but he gives feedback in a way that tells you he really cares. You know he's doing it because he wants you to be the best you can be. That's what we all need, honest feedback, even when it's uncomfortable.

When I came into the business, I told Todd; If I'm doing anything that you don't think I should do, tell me, keep me on track. He asked for and I gave him permission to be tough. I do the same thing today; I ask permission, "May I give you some honest feedback if I see you getting off track?" Sometimes, as a coach, you have to be tough.

When Doug and Cliff and I came into the business, Todd told us, "When I come to Fargo, if you do not have 30 last names in the room, I'm not coming back, and they cannot be friends and relatives unless they are sharp." We knew he was serious, we had over 30 last names in the room and he did come back. If we had come up short, he would have stuck to his word, if not, everything else he told us would have meant nothing.

Be a student of the industry. Never stop learning. Commit yourself to constant improvement. I believe that this one single point is worth all the rest.

Seek first to understand, then to be understood.
Stephen Covey

John, is it true that you gave Peter Fonda a tape?

Evidence Of Leadership

What was the evidence that told you that you were becoming a leader?

It was a lot of little things, things like conducting a meeting and having people whom I perceived to be much more successful than I, asking my advice. You sit back and you wonder, "Imagine her, as successful as she is, asking me a maintenance manager, (as I still pictured myself), asking my advice!"

One of the most visible and thrilling examples of my financial success was the time we sold our trailer for $1,800. An $1,800 trailer gives you a good idea of where we came from.

Another high point in Rexall Showcase International was my third corporate conference in Nashville, Tennessee. I had been in the business a year and a half and this was the first conference my wife attended with me. Damon DeSantis put on a black tie dinner for us. Here I was with twenty of the top people in the company. My wife was in a formal gown, I was in a tuxedo, and we were picked up in a long black limousine and driven to a mystery dinner. I remember walking into this big museum-house-mansion in Nashville. Everyone was talking about Peter Fonda, I'm asking, "Who's Peter Fonda?" As I walk in the door, I shake this guy's hand and I said, "Where's Peter Fonda?" He said, "I'm Peter Fonda!" There is no doubt that we were hicks. This whole conference just blew my wife away, now she began to believe in the business.

I was asked to speak in front of 3,000 people and when I spoke I got caught up in my speech. I talked about my belief that commitment and personal growth were responsible for 80% of my success. I talked about having to pay the price.

A strange thing happened to me as I was speaking, I certainly did not plan on this happening. I started talking about my dyslexia and my problems as a child being unable to read. This was the first time anyone in my organization heard that I had this problem. No one knew I could not read, not my upline, not my downline, not my sponsor. It blew people away. I got a standing ovation and came close to celebrity status from that point forward. After that conference, everywhere I went people wanted to talk to me. This speech was a major turning point. Looking back I can understand that my story empowered others. We all love to see the underdog overcome huge challenges and win. The Rocky movies are an example of this.

A few years later we went up another notch. We sold our home, bought a lake home on one of the nicest lakes in Minnesota and planned to spend the winters in San Diego. It turned out that we preferred the Minnesota / North Dakota area. We moved back to Fargo and kept our lake home.

Four Stages of Growth

As distributors we go through four stages in our growth:

Unconscious Incompetent:

Imagine a very young child who has to have his shoes tied up for him. He does not know how to tie his shoes and he does not know that he does not know how to tie them.

As unconscious incompetents we have no idea what we're doing and the worst part is that we don't know, what we don't know.

Conscious Incompetent:

Now the young child knows that he has to have his shoes tied for him. If you ask him if he can tie his own shoes he will tell you that he does not know how.

As Conscious Incompetents we suddenly realize that we don't know what we're doing. If we are honest we will call on others who do know what they are doing and can do it better than we can.

Conscious Competent:

Now the child knows how to tie his own shoes. If you ask him if he can tie his own shoes he will be very proud to tell you and to show you just how well he can do it.

As conscious competents we say to ourselves, "I'm getting a handle on this, I can do it, in fact I'm getting pretty good at it.

Unconscious Competent:

Now the young child knows how to ties his own shoes and he does it as he listens to the radio, talks on the phone to his best friend and tells his mother that he really is cleaning up his room. He has become an unconscious competent, he can tie his shoes without thinking about it, almost without being aware that he is tying his shoes.

As unconscious competents we do the right thing and say the right things automatically. If I ask Janie Fischer to do a three-way-call she will know exactly what to say and when to say it. She will not have to think about it, it will be automatic.

Janie will be the first one to tell you that it was not always this way with her. Like the rest of us she started as an unconscious incompetent and worked her way up through the four stages to become the professional network marketing success that she is today.

Ask Randy Schroeder about his first Rexall presentation or better still listen to his own description on his Recruit tape. Randy will tell you that the knowing comes in the doing. Do the thing and you will learn how to do it.

The knowing comes in the doing.
Randy Schroeder

I reached a point, after we bought our lake home, that I was comfortable, maybe too comfortable. The money kept coming in no matter what I did day to day. I backed off a little. I didn't work as hard as I did in the past and I got stagnant as a leader. My saga began to fade.

It took me awhile, but I found that when I'm working, when I'm growing, when I'm learning, when I'm out on the hunt, talking to people, this is when I come alive. It took me a year and a half to get back, to get the feeling back. I'm sure the leaders in the company thought that I had gone into retirement.

At our corporate conference in Orlando, Florida, I retold my story. The response was the same as the first time, a standing ovation. I know that my story empowers people and I have found my passion. This conference rekindled my burning desire to "Go to the Top", to grow and to be all that I can be.

These were the significant events that were turning points for me.

Trailer for sale $1500

The view in Hong Kong. "Things never looked like this in the maintenance department."

Accomplishments

What is your proudest accomplishment?

Probably the speech I gave at our corporate conference in Orlando. The theme of the talk was "I'm going to the top". I told my story of overcoming the challenges of severe dyslexia and extremely low self-esteem. Whenever I tell this story I feel the pain and the shame I endured all through grade school and high school but I know my story empowers others by showing them that they can overcome the challenges we all face in network marketing.

I am proud of the things I did as a Maintenance Manager, the things I built and the systems I designed and installed. Most of them are still working today. When you put in a hard day's work it gives you get a real sense of accomplishment.

It's different in networking marketing. You're working hard; you're putting your energy in. You might work for a week and get paid for a day. You might work for a month and get paid for an hour. In traditional business you work for a day and you get paid for a day. You can measure your success by your paycheck on a day-to-day business. In network marketing that's not the case. Measure your accomplishments each day by the seeds you sow not by the crops you harvest.

Measure every day's accomplishments by the seeds sown not by the crops harvested.
Earl Nightingale

Todd Smith says there are three stages you go through in network marketing:

- first you're underpaid,

- then you're paid what you're worth,

- eventually you're paid far more than anyone's worth

It's tough to get through that first underpaid stage. Tom Bissmeyer says "The first $5,000 you earn in this business will be the toughest $5,000 you will ever earn". You have to hold the vision and continue to move forward.

My proudest accomplishment in network marketing is in seeing the development of other people. Knowing where I've come from, to see other people growing, to see that sparkle in their eye and to see them transform as a person, is the ultimate feeling of accomplishment. It is exciting to see others alive and well and loving what they are doing. Life itself will beat the daylights out of you and network marketing seems to breathe it back in. It gives you a rebirth of hope. It feels good. You feel good. This is what gives a leader an overwhelming sense of accomplishment.

I've said it before, and I'll say it again:

There's no business, no profession and no activity more noble than that of encouraging the development of people.

What would you have done differently?

Distributors ask me, "John, what are the keys to success in Rexall Showcase International"?

The first key is personal growth: I believe that personal growth is responsible for 80% of your success. Become worth more. Become the leader you must become to lead your team with vision, courage and integrity.

The second thing is that most of us spend our time with the wrong people: You can waste an entire year with the wrong person. It is not that we don't care about everybody, not that we don't want everybody to succeed. Trying to help someone do this business who is not ready or doesn't want to make the effort, is like trying to make a pig fly. It's going to frustrate you and frustrate the pig because the pig is not going to fly. The same thing happens when you try to help someone do this business who is not ready to do the business.

The secret is in spending time with the right people. Work with your leaders and with your distributors that have the potential and the desire to be leaders. If one of your distributors is coachable, following the system and working hard, spend your time with them. The longer you are in the business, the better you become at identifying these winners.

I would definitely have spent my time better by working with the right people.

You must first be a believer if you
want to be an achiever.
Anonymous

We can't direct the wind but
we can adjust the sails.
Anonymous

You are the architect of
your personal experience.
Shirley MacLaine

I discovered I always have choices and
sometimes it's only a choice of attitude.
Judith M. Knowlton

CHAPTER 8

In the Right Business, Doing the Wrong Things

John, we've been talking about doing the right things. What are some of the biggest mistakes we make as distributors, particularly when we're new in the business?

Spending time with the wrong people: Undoubtedly, the biggest mistake we make, not just as new distributors but even after we been in the business for a long time, is that we spend time with the wrong people. I still find myself falling into this trap. You can't push a rope. We want it more for some distributors than they want it for themselves. I'm not suggesting that you forget anyone because everyone's important, everyone adds up. You must match energy with energy.

"There are three secrets of managing distributors, unfortunately no one knows what they are." Big Al

---

In the land of the blind the one-eyed man is king.

The story is told of a guest who arrived at a large and very ornate lodge. After checking in and leaving her bags in her room she went back down to the lobby. A very congenial stranger approached the guest in the lobby and asked if she would like a tour of the lodge. She was delighted and spent the next hour touring the lodge with the stranger. The stranger seemed to know everything about the lodge from the beach area to the golf course and everything in-between.

When they arrived back at the lobby the guest thanked the stranger for the tour and remarked that he must have been there for a long time to know the lodge so well. The stranger's response was interesting, "Oh no, I'm a guest here too, I just arrived yesterday".

By the time you get on-board with Rexall Showcase International you will know far more than you realize. Start from there. You will learn as you earn. As Randy Schroeder says "The knowing comes in the doing, activity generates knowledge".

Get started with what you know. Get your goals down on paper, write your warm list of 100 people, get tapes out and use your upline. You will be amazed at how much you learn as you listen in on three-way calls, listen to your upline, listen to tapes and attend every event you can.

The key thing is to get started, get going now.

Thinking that we need to know everything: Another mistake we make is thinking that we need to know everything. It's not knowledge that generates activity; it's activity that generates knowledge. We learn by doing. Distributors enter this business, particularly from the sales world, and they think they need to know everything: The ins and outs of the compensation plan and everything about the products. The problem is, everything you do in this business sets an example on how and what your people will do. If you go out there and talk like a product expert or a compensation expert, your people will they think they have to be experts. You may impress them and they may decide that they could never do what you do, that they could never know as much as you. Everything you do in the process of recruiting is setting an example, showing your people what they have to do to be successful.

Don't confuse activity with accomplishment: We often confuse activity, being busy, with accomplishment. There we are, we're busy, busy, busy all the time, but are we really getting anything done? Don't confuse pay-time activity with no pay time activity. The thing that new distributors get paid for is talking to someone who is not in the business. That's what they get paid for. It may be for someone you want to recruit on your front line or it may be for someone in your downline but as new distributors we get paid only for talking to someone who is not in the business. In his tape Recruit - the Only Way to Success, Randy Schroeder says that until we are earning $5,000 a month, 100% of our time should be spent on recruiting. Someone else in your upline is being paid to teach and train your new distributors.

The skill to do comes in the doing.
Randy Schroeder

No pay-time is all the other activities we love such as, organizing our files, reading the literature, watching the product video for the 12th time, good stuff, but it will not add a nickel to our next commission check.

Pay time is time spent talking to someone who is not in the business.

The 90/10 rule: I learned this rule from Dr. Neil Secrist one weekend at my lake home. Neil heard it from Richard Epley, who heard it on a flight from an Amway Crown Ambassador. Richard asked the Ambassador, "Can you give me one piece of advice"? The Crown Ambassador said, "Understand that 90% of everything we do, the money we invest and the time we spend, is wasted. It's the 10% that will make us wealthy beyond our dreams. The problem is that we don't know what the 90% is and the 10% is so we have to do it all."

The next time you're down or frustrated remember the 90/10 rule. You're doing a meeting and no one showed up. You travelled across town to meet someone and they didn't show up, they didn't call to cancel and then they didn't even call to apologize. One of your key leaders or potential leaders quits the business and you had your heart set on what they could do. These are all part of the 90%, keep on doing the right things, they will include the 10% that will make you wealthy beyond your dreams.

90% of everything you do is wasted, 10% will make you wealthy beyond your dreams.

Early in my Rexall Showcase International career I flew to a city to meet with and do a meeting for a new distributor. Not only did he not show up at the airport, I never heard from him again. That was part of the 90%.

Don't prejudge people: We have no way of knowing who will be or who won't be right and ready for the business. Every dud knows a stud. Everyone deserves a chance to say no. It is not our job to judge anyone, to decide for anyone. It is our job to get the information in front of anybody and everybody and let them make the decision. We do not have a magic wand that we can wave over people and know if they will be a stud or a dud.

Missing events: Not everyone who comes to the meetings or to every event makes $10,000 a month, but I can tell you that anybody making $10,000 a month is at every event. You need to be there. These events are a part of our lives. If you've had a good day, the meeting needs you. If you've had a bad day, you need the meeting.

We all talk too much:
Read this phrase out loud. Burn it into your memory.

Say less to more people.

One of the biggest challenges we have, especially those who have had experience in sales, is that they talk too much. Good communication is listening 70% of the time. Most of us talk 70% of the time and more, much more.

It is not our job to judge anyone, to decide for anyone. It is our job to get information in front of anybody and everybody and let them make their own decision.

Management mode: We go out and sponsor a few people, now we want to manage them. The problem is that out of ten people only one or two will do something. Maybe none of them will do anything, we don't know, remember the 90/10 rule. Keep sponsoring. Keep out in front of the pack. Keep out performing the rest of your people. You will be setting the example, the right example. If you fall into a management role your distributors will do the same. Soon everybody will be sitting there trying to manage the last new person who came in, trying to get that person to do something.

Lone Rangers lose: This business is not like the old movies where the Lone Ranger rides into town, shoots all the bad guys, cleans up the town, rescues the lady in distress and rides off into the sunset. In our business lone rangers lose. Your upline is there to be to be used. They are being paid to help you be successful. Think of them as successful consultants, available on demand, at no cost, free. Your sponsor wants to hear from you. If your sponsor doesn't hear from you, he or she will assume that you're not doing the business. This is a business of team effort. You must employ the team because you'll never be able to build a large organization without help, without having your upline work with you.

Don't reinvent the wheel: We have a proven system. It works. If it worked for thousands and thousands of RSI distributors, do you think it will work for you?

Not too long ago a guy came into the business with a sales background and told me, "John, you've done great. But I'm here now. I'll show you how this should be done." My response was, "You know what, Joe? I've made $1.5 million doing it this way. Why don't we try it this way first?" Don't reinvent the wheel.

Say less to more people.

Say less to more people.

Say less to more people.

Say less to more people.

Say less to more people.

Say less to more people.

Say less to more people.

Say less to more people.

Say less to more people.

Your living is determined not so much by what life brings you as by the attitude you bring to life; not so much by what happens to you as by the way your mind looks at what happens.
John Homer Miller

Attitude = Success
John Berta

CHAPTER 9

Your Why &
Setting Goals

John what is the starting point in this business?

What is your why? The starting point is knowing why you want to get involved with Rexall Showcase. There is nothing as important as identifying your "WHY."

Why did you sign-up?	Why RSI?
Why are you doing the business?	Why RSI products?
Why will you drive you for success?	

If you do not have a strong "WHY", you will not be around long enough to learn the "HOW" of doing the business.

If you are a normal human being there will be numerous times when you will feel like quitting. Your WHY will be your rock and your stay. Your WHY will keep you in the business. It will give you the courage and the will to continue when everything that can go wrong has gone wrong.

Establish your "WHY", get it in writing, keep it in front of you and review it often. Your WHY is the big picture, it is your desired end result. Stephen Covey talks about the need to "begin with the end in mind". What is your end in mind? Get a clear image, a vision. What will you be doing when you reach your WHY? Where will you be? Who will be there with you? What will you be doing? What will you be wearing? Visualize your WHY at least once a day.

What is the difference between your why's and your goals?

A why is very general such as, "I am determined to achieve financial independence", or "I want to spend more time with my family". It may me "I want to get out of this rat race and do what is important to me, where I want to do it, when I want to do it, with whom I want to do it".

A goal should be a specific target such as, "I am committed to build my Rexall Showcase International monthly income to $3,000 a month by December 31 of this year" or "I will allocate from 5:00 to 8:00 every day to spend time with my family".

Some goals should be specific activities such as, "I will get two tapes out every day before I go to bed".

Once you have your WHY firmly established you will need to have a plan of action and goals, stepping stones, to get there. Many of us set unrealistic goals; this can be a destructive exercise. Goals are meant to be tough and challenging but attainable. They should not be easy; you should have to stretch to reach them.

Comfortable = Broke
John Berta

This is my why:

_____

_____

_____

_____

_____

_____

_____

_____

If you do not have a WHY, you will
never learn the HOW.

Talk to me about goals. Are goals all that important?

I believe that the problem is not in achieving our goals, it is in identifying and setting our goals. Setting goals can be scary, subconsciously you have made a commitment and you risk letting yourself down.

In this business you must have goals, business goals that fit with your life goals.

One of the goal-setting techniques I use is Zig Ziglar's. He has an entire videotape on setting goals. The following is a summary:

- Identify each goal and set a date, a deadline for achieving it.

- List the benefits. What will your life be like when you achieve your goal.

- List the obstacles, the challenges, in attaining that goal.

- Identify the people, the places and the things that will help you achieve your goal.

- List the knowledge or the skills that you need to attain to achieve your goal.

- Develop a plan of action, be very specific.

Start your goal setting exercise with a dream sheet. List everything you would like to have, to own or to do. Don't hold back; don't compromise, list everything.

As you're setting a goal, be specific and realistic about the goal. Review and update your goals on a regular basis. As Brian Tracy says, "Inspect what you expect", or as Stewart Hughes says, "When performance is measured, performance improves".

In network marketing, your goals must be specific and based on the day-to-day activities. They must include how many tapes you're going to get out, how many follow-up calls you will make, how many three-way calls you're going to do.

You also need long range goals, when are you going to become a Director, when are you going to reach Century Elect? When are you going to reach the Century Club? These goals should be complimentary with what you and your family want to accomplish in life.

Goals must be in writing. They must be detailed, specific, reviewed and updated. I believe that if a goal is not in writing, it is nothing more than a wish. Someone said, "If you want your dreams to come true, you must first wake up." The first step in moving from a dream to a goal is to get it down on paper.

Use the following pages as a guide to setting your major goals. These may be physical, spiritual, career, financial or family goals. Make a few copies of these pages before you fill them in so that you can review and revise your goals on a regular basis.

The following is Zig Ziglar's goal setting guide from his book "Over the Top", published by Thomas Nelson Publishers, Nashville.

GOAL SETTING – EXAMPLE 1

Step 1 What is my goal?

I want to earn $5,000 a month from RSI.

Step 2 My benefits from reaching this goal.

We will not have to be concerned about money ever again. We can buy a new car. We can add a family room to our home.

Step 3 What challenges must I overcome?

Right now we are just barely getting by and I don't know where I will find the money to do the business. I have no time, I work hard 8 hours a day, I have two little characters at home to take care of and I have a busy social life.

Step 4 What skills do I need?

The skill to manage my time better, to make priorities and get them done first. I must learn how to present the RSI story without talking too much. I will have to learn the discipline of getting tapes out on a regular basis despite my busy life and all the distractions I face.

Step 5 Who Can Assist Me?

My sponsor Pat was in the same situation as me just two years ago, she has promised to help me. Pat's sponsor Jim has been very supportive already and he has promised to help. Todd Smith through his tapes.

Step 6 What is my plan of action?

I will mail out at least 1 tape every day.
I will make 3 follow up calls every day.
I will talk to Pat at least 3 times a week and to Jim once a week.
I will be at the next corporate conference.

Step 7 What is my completion date?

I will be at $2,000 by Dec 31,_____

GOAL SETTING - EXAMPLE 2

Step 1 What is my goal?

I want to spend 4 hours a day with my family.

Step 2 My benefits from reaching this goal.

I will be much closer to my children. I will be more involved in their lives.

Step 3 What challenges must I overcome?

I'm so busy already that I feel as if I don't give my kids the attention they deserve. When I do spend time with my kids I'm so tired that I can't really give them my full attention. How can I ever find time to do the business?

Step 4 What skills do I need?

I need to learn to say no to things that will not help be achieve my goals. I need to learn how to focus on what I'm doing and not get distracted by other things. I need to learn how to allocate time with my kids and not let anything interfere.

Step 5 Who Can Assist Me?

Pat has 3 kids in grade school and somehow she found time to do the business. I'm going to take a time management course. I have started using a day planner to organize myself. Jim promised to coach me for the next 90 days.

Step 6 What is my plan of action?

I will block off from 6:00 to 8:00 every night to be with my kids. I will keep every Sat afternoon free for my kids.

Step 7 What is my completion date?

I have already started this plan. I will review it at least once a month.
My kids know my plan. They will tell me how I'm doing.

GOAL 1

Step 1 What is my goal?

_____

_____

Step 2 My benefits from reaching this goal.

_____

_____

_____

_____

Step 3 What challenges must I overcome?

_____

_____

_____

_____

Step 4 What skills do I need?

_____

_____

Step 5 Who Can Assist Me?

_____

_____

Step 6 What is my plan of action?

_____

_____

_____

Step 7 What is my completion date?

_____

_____

GOAL 2

Step 1 What is my goal?

_____

_____

Step 2 My benefits from reaching this goal.

_____

_____

_____

_____

Step 3 What challenges must I overcome?

_____

_____

_____

_____

Step 4 What skills do I need?

_____

_____

Step 5 Who Can Assist Me?

_____

_____

Step 6 What is my plan of action?

_____

_____

_____

Step 7 What is my completion date?

_____

_____

GOAL 3

Step 1 What is my goal?

Step 2 My benefits from reaching this goal.

Step 3 What challenges must I overcome?

Step 4 What skills do I need?

Step 5 Who Can Assist Me?

Step 6 What is my plan of action?

Step 7 What is my completion date?

GOAL 4

Step 1 What is my goal?

Step 2 My benefits from reaching this goal.

Step 3 What challenges must I overcome?

Step 4 What skills do I need?

Step 5 Who Can Assist Me?

Step 6 What is my plan of action?

Step 7 What is my completion date?

Stewart Hughes used lines from Thomas S. Monson to introduce a theme at the Long Beach Conference in 1998.

These lines can have a profound impact on our business every day, day-in and day-out.

---

*When we deal in generalities we
shall never succeed.
When we deal in specifics we shall
rarely have a failure.
When performance is measured,
performance improves,
When performance is measured and reported
back the rate of improvement accelerates.*

These are the questions we must ask ourselves;

Am I dealing in generalities such as?

- I want to earn more money.

- I want to spend more time with my family.

- I want to add a few more people to my front line.

Am I dealing in specifics such as?

- I will be at $3,000 a month by December 31

- I will dedicate three hours a day to my family from 5:00 to 8:00 PM everyday.

- I will be at every one of my children's events.

- I will add three distributors to my front line by June of this year.

Am I measuring my performance?

- Do I know how many tapes I sent out yesterday, last week, and last month?

- Do I know how many follow up calls I made yesterday, last week, and last month?

- Do I know how many tapes got listened to?

Who do I report my performance to?

- When was the last time I spoke to my sponsor?

- Did I review my plans with my sponsor?

- Did I tell my sponsor what I did last week?

- Is there someone in my upline who would be willing to coach me?

- Would he or she be as tough as Todd Smith?

- If they agreed to coach me would I accept their coaching? Would I do what they suggested I do?

It's not what happens to you, it's what you do about it.
W Mitchell

The pessimist sees difficulty in every opportunity.
The optimist sees opportunity in every difficulty.
Winston Churchill

Either I will find a way or I will make one.
P. Sidney

CHAPTER 10

Affirmations

John how did you keep your belief up, how did you keep going through your first few tough months?

I believe an important point in staying focused and attaining your goals is the use of affirmations. An affirmation is a positive statement about something you wish to embed deeply into your subconscious mind. Thanks to Todd Smith there are a few affirmations that have become familiar to many Rexall Showcase International distributors.

- Discipline is doing, what you know you should do, when you know you should do it, whether you feel like it or not.

- I do things one at a time until I'm done.

- I always do, what I said I would do, when I said I would do it.

One of the phrases that is well known through "Think and Grow Rich" by Napoleon Hill is, "If you can control your mind, you can control your destiny here on this earth." Essentially, we are what we think about.

How important is it to control our self-talk? Negative self-talk is one of the biggest challenges we all face, it's that little thing inside that says, "Don't do it, you'll look ridiculous, you can't, you're crazy, what will your friends say, what will your colleagues think." Our whole world is flooded with negative news, negative information. Does, "CNN stand for Constant Negative News"? How can you control negative self-talk so that you don't buy into it? You must flood yourself with positive information.

John, how do you flood yourself with positive information? What techniques do you use?

I love to listen to audiotapes. I remember times when I would leave Denver, Colorado after an evening business briefing and drive back to Fargo, a 13-hour drive. I'd drive all night listening to tapes and I would be on fire by the time I got home. I would be elated because the tapes reinforced that I was headed in the right direction. They helped me to understand what successful people do and what unsuccessful people do. As Jim Rohn says, "Find out what unsuccessful people do and don't do it."

Instead of reading a newspaper in the morning, read a motivational book or a book on network marketing, listen to a motivational tape or review your goals. Do you think that would change your life instead of reading the news or watching TV?

Find out what unsuccessful
people do and don't do it.
Jim Rohn

Do you have time to do it? The average person in America spends 30 hours a week watching TV. They drive 18,000 miles a year, 700 hours a year in their car. You could learn how to do brain surgery in 700 hours. People say they don't have time for this stuff, it's really a matter of making time and making it your priority. Make your car a university on wheels. Take advantage of every spare minute to put the good stuff in, to build your knowledge and your self-esteem. I guarantee that a commitment to do this will change your life.

I can't afford all those books and tapes: There is a wealth of this information available at most libraries. No, they don't deliver, you'll have to go down and get it.

Create your own list of positive affirmations that will keep you headed in the right direction. Keep them in front of you, around your house, in the bathroom, on the dashboard of your car, in your day timer, on your desk. Keep them wherever you can see them often. They will help to keep your attitude positive. I have heard that 87% of our self-talk is negative. (I always wondered how they measure something like that.)

Positive affirmations are the best way to keep negative self-talk at bay. As Zig Ziglar says, "Keep putting the good stuff in", this way there will be no room for the bad stuff, like those nagging doubts that plague us.

Keep putting the good stuff in.
Zig Ziglar

These are the affirmations I live with.

- Happiness is an inside job.

- We are what we think about.

- You can diffuse any argument by just agreeing.

- Don't worry about what other people are thinking or doing.

- You and only you can make changes

- Take responsibility for yourself

- Be a do it now person, don't procrastinate

- I have a win, win attitude

- You will not win by being defensive

- COMMITMENT is doing what you said you were going to do long after the feeling you felt when you said you were going to do it has gone.

- Good attitudes find solutions, bad attitudes find excuses

- You teach more by what you do than by what you say.

- Don't confuse activity with accomplishment

- You can't get to second with your foot on first

- Do I work when I work?

"Its not what you earn, its what you become in the process."
Jim Rohn on earning your first million dollars.

Stewart Hughes on affirmations, visualization and goals.

On one of his leadership tapes Stewart Hughes gives us an excellent illustration of the power of affirmations, visualization and setting goals. Stewart was a young man earning $300 a week selling life insurance. His manager came to him one week and said "Listen, we've got a guy coming in from Canada that's going to change your life." He will be doing a series of seminars, one day a week for four weeks. The cost was $200; however, the manager agreed to pay up front and to take $10 a month out of Stewart's paycheck until it was paid up.

Stewart says, "The speaker was Bob Proctor from Toronto, Canada. He was a great seminar speaker. He had me turned on, motivated, I was excited. He changed my life.

At the end of the four weeks he said if you take what you really want to have happen in your life, write it down on this card, put it in this plastic pouch and carry it around with you it will happen. I said, that's easy, no problem, I'll do that. I wrote down that I wanted to be a Vice President, earning $100,000 a year by the time I was 30. I carried it around in my pocket for a couple of years and it didn't work. I worked hard but it didn't happen, so I threw the thing away.

I woke up one morning six years later, at 27 years old and realized that I was earning $100,000 a year as a Vice President of E.F.Hutton. I said, Stewart, it worked. Why did it work? I have now read over 200 books on the subject. Over the years I have refined the process. Realize that the will, willpower, by itself, will not do it for you, you must employ the power of your subconscious mind."

Work is either fun or drudgery.
It depends on your attitude. I like fun.
Colleen Barrett

Our life is a reflection of our attitudes.
Anonymous

Enthusiasm is the little thing that
makes a big difference.
Anonymous

CHAPTER 11

Enjoy the Journey

John I know that when you first got involved in network marketing you were excited about the income opportunities. How did you feel about the business itself? Did you enjoy the process of recruiting, building and nurturing?

I have a feeling that this will be the shortest and the most important chapter in the book. The answer is that I loved the process from day one. This does not mean that I did not have bad days and tough times; they come with the territory.

I believe that to be successful in Rexall Showcase International you must love what you're doing, you must enjoy the process of building your business. The very pursuit of our goals should give us something we want. The goal is important and the process of working toward that goal must give us a sense of satisfaction.

The pursuit and the process are more important than the result.

To be successful in our business you must love the process of meeting people and leading them. I loved this aspect of the business from the day I got involved. I still find it to be the most rewarding part of the business.

We can get so caught up in the pursuit of our goals that we overlook the simple pleasures of doing the business. We are changing lives. We are introducing people to a way of life that sets them free from the tyranny of maxed out credit cards, 9:00-to-whatever days and the constant threat of being reorganized right out of a job. We are making it possible for parents to put their children first and to organize their days around their children's events. We are presenting a lifestyle that takes families back to the days of self-sufficiency, financial independence and having meals together around the family table.

When you find value in the process you will not feel the sacrifices along the way. The secret is to find pleasure in and believe in what you're doing.

Imagine that you are meeting with a prospect for the first time. If your concentration is on how this prospect will move you closer to your goal when you sign them up as a director, you will not be effective and you will certainly not be successful in the long-term. If you are totally focused on the prospect, on his or her goals, on the lifestyle that they can live, then you are on the right track. Show your prospect how much you care about their concerns, their priorities, their lifestyle.

The secret is to find pleasure in and believe in
what you're doing every day.

Enjoy the Journey

- Love the pursuit.

- Live in the present.

- Enjoy the process.

- Focus on the task at hand.

- Be committed to right now, to this minute.

- Wherever you are – be there.

- Love what you do and do what you love.

- Understand the lifestyle you are presenting. Remember that you are freeing people from dead end jobs, from the tyranny of maxed out credit cards, from the rat race that condemns people and families to lives of quiet desperation. You are involved in a noble profession. There's no business, no profession and no activity more noble than that of encouraging the development of people.

Find within the process and the pursuit, the pleasures that will make ever day a winner.

*The great at anything do not set to work
because they are inspired but rather become
inspired because they are working. They don't
waste time waiting for inspiration.*

Ernest Newman

Getting Started on the Journey

The longest journey begins with a single step.

I became a human tape dispenser.
If it moved, I'd give it a tape.
If it didn't move, I'd kick it, then if
it moved, I'd give it a tape.

I've never met a person,
I don't care what his condition,
in whom I could not see possibilities.
I don't care how much a man may consider
himself a failure, I believe in him, for he can
change the thing that is wrong in his life any
time he is ready and prepared to do it.
Whenever he develops the desire, he can take
away from his life the thing that is defeating
it. The capacity for reformation
and change lies within.

Preston Bradley

CHAPTER 12

The Process of Sponsoring

John if you were to go out today to sponsor more distributors, how would you go about it, what would you do?

Sponsoring, bringing someone into the business is not an event, it is a process. It is a series of events that lead to the individual saying "Yes, count me in." or saying, "No, its not right for me at this time in my life." Sponsoring is a process of exposure, getting and keeping information in front of the prospect.

The process through which I have been successful in building my business is using an audiotape as the individual's first exposure to Rexall Showcase International. Let me caution you that the audiotape is not designed to sell the opportunity, it is designed to get an appointment. It's designed to get you face-to-face with the prospect so that you can answer their questions. It's designed to create curiosity. An audiotape is a very efficient, non-threatening, non-confrontational way to get information in front of others without wasting your time or the prospect's time. They can listen while they're driving, while they're stuck in traffic or when they are doing any activity that does not demand their full attention. You're not driving for 20 minutes and spending an hour with someone to find out if they have an interest or not. When an audiotape is used correctly it is an effective way of getting information in front of someone who may be interested.

The Audio Tape

- It always gives a perfect presentation.

- It can give the perfect presentation over and over as many times as the prospect wishes.

- It does not waste your prospect's time.

- It uses down time, such as driving time.

- It does not waste your time. You do not have to spend time with someone who is not interested in the business.

- It does a much better job than you can do personally unless you can bring along three or four doctors, a few lawyers and a few entrepreneurs all of whom have a track record of success in the business.

- It is a very cost-effective tool. For $1.00 and postage you hired a group of successful professionals to present your case. They will present it as many times as requested.

- It is non-confrontational. If you give it to a friend and the friend says "no", they are saying "no" to a tape not to you personally. It does not impact on your relationship. It opens the door for you to make an appointment.

What is the most important function of the audiotape?

- … It identifies people who are not interested so that you do not have to spend time with them……….

The tape has limitations:

- It is not you. It can never convey the enthusiasm, the belief that you have in Rexall Showcase International.

- It has no personality. It cannot adapt its story to the interests of the listener.

- It cannot make an appointment. It can only open the door for you to make an appointment.

People ask me, "What was your plan? What was your strategy?" My business plan was very simple. I became a human tape dispenser. If it moved, I'd give it a tape. If it didn't move, I'd kick it, then if it moved, I'd give it a tape. It comes back to the pipeline principle, if you get enough people to look at the company, the products and the income potential some will want to know more. This opens the door.

On a few occasions when I had an individual that was a 9 or 10 on my scale of 1 to 10, I would meet with the individual for coffee and give them the tape personally. I explained how the tape system works and I told them that normally I would have sent them the tape in the mail but I wanted to have coffee with them and explain the system.

This is a two-step process.

(1) We get the information out in front of others through an audiotape in the mail or meeting with them one-on-one.

(2) We follow up and one of three things will happen:

- "Thanks but no thanks". This is not for everyone.

- "I'm not interested in the business, but I want to try the products." We can sell them product from our inventory or have it shipped directly from the RSI.

- "Tell me more this sounds interesting". Now we take them to the next step.

The Follow-up Script

Your initial follow up call should be very brief and to the point. This is not the time to talk about the weather, last night's big game or your mother-in-law. To be effective use a script. If you don't like this one, make up your own.

Your conversation should go something like this:

Peter, I sent you a tape, did you get it?	Yes John I did.
Did you get a chance to listen to it?	Yes I did.
Would you like to know more?	Yes I would.
What did you like best about the tape?	

If Peter replies, "Yes" to the third question, your response is "What did you like best about the tape?" not, "Did you like the tape?"

This little bit of phrasing can make a big difference. Now the prospect has to think, "What did I like best about the tape?"

You may be a brilliant conversationalist and be able to handle your calls without a script. What happens to your new distributor who does not have your gift of gab? What happens when your new distributor stumbles and fumbles through their first few follow up calls?

They get discouraged and they quit. When you ask why they quit, they tell you that they just do not have your conversational skills.

If you follow a script, you will be more effective. Your distributors will follow a script and they will be more effective. Do you have a better idea?

When the prospect is interested in knowing more you can take one of four approaches.

(A) **You can meet with them one-on-one:** If you're brand new in the business and if your sponsor is local have your sponsor come with you. A two-on-one presentation is much more effective than a one-on-one. First the prospect learns about the business from your sponsor who has been in the business longer than you have. Second you learn the business by watching your sponsor and listening to the questions they ask. Third and this may be by far the most important dynamic of the meeting, your prospect sees the support and says, "This support is very good, I can do this, I can bring my friends to a friendly, informal meeting like this". This is a key dynamic of a two-on-one meeting.

Doug Overvold is insistent that the best step after a tape is always to get together face-to-face with the prospect. In Doug's opinion the prospect is buying you as much as they are buying Rexall Showcase International and they will never see you through a video.

This was Doug's response on why he prefers to meet face-to-face with the prospect as soon as possible:

"There are several factors. The first is that this is a relationship business. I have found that one of the best ways to build relationships is to ask questions. It is through these questions that you build rapport and find out what the prospect is really looking for. My favorite question is 'What do you know about network marketing, are your feelings positive, neutral or negative'? The key is to listen and understand how the person is really feeling. In my opinion, right now, this is the most effective approach."

The Three Way Script

Initial follow-up call

When you are new in the business it is a good idea to have your sponsor on the line when you are making your initial follow-up calls.

Peter, I sent you a tape, did you get it?	Yes John I did.
Did you get a chance to listen to it?	Yes I did.
Would you like to know more?	Yes I would.
What did you like best about the tape?	
My associate Neil Roth is on the line, he has been helping me with my follow up calls. Neil has been in the business for several years and he is better positioned to answer any questions you may have. Do you have a minute to talk to him"?	Sure, go ahead.
"Peter meet my colleague Neil Roth from Las Vegas.	

This is where you stop talking .... shut up ..... don't talk any more ... keep quiet .... don't say another word until your sponsor requests it.

The Three Way Script

Second follow-up call

In this example you called your prospect earlier and they expressed interest in the business. You arranged to call them back and introduce them to your colleague in Rexall Showcase International.

Is Peter there?	This is Peter.
Peter the last time we talked I promised to introduce you to my associate in Rexall Showcase International. Do you have a few minutes now?	Yes I do.
"Peter, I would like to introduce you to my sponsor Neil Roth from Las Vegas. Neil has been in the business for several years and he is better positioned to answer any questions you may have. Neil meet Peter."	

This is where you stop talking .... shut up ..... don't talk any more ... keep quiet .... don't say another word until your sponsor requests it.

What are the dynamics of the three-way process?

- The first dynamic is third-party validation. Someone else verifies the story.

- The second dynamic is the learning experience for the new distributor because the information is passing through their ears as well as the prospect's ears so they learn how to tell the story.

- The unspoken message is that help is available. The distributor is not alone, they have support. They don't have to do it on their own. This is a powerful subconscious message. The prospect says, "This is simple, I can do this."

(B) **You can use a three-way call as the next step:** Whether this is the next step or comes later in the cycle, do not skip the three-way call. It has the same dynamic as a two-on-one meeting. It's third-party validation, someone else to verify the story. There's an old saying: "If one person says it, it may be true, if two people say it, it's got to be true."

A three-way call is as simple as having your sponsor on the line when you do your follow-up call on the prospect. You introduce your sponsor to your prospect and then you stop talking. Please see the suggested script.

(C) **You can send the prospect a package:** You can send the prospect a package of information containing a video, the Rexall Showcase International Corporate Profile brochure and a few more tapes. The advantages of this approach are that it further qualifies the individual. Once they have seen the video they will know a lot more about the company, the products, the compensation plan and the investment required. This can save you a great deal of time. Once they have seen the video they are much better informed and in a much better position to make their decision.

Neil Roth uses this approach exclusively. Neil works out of Las Vegas and has built an organization in 38 states and three countries by using this follow-up package. If the prospect is interested, Neil sends them a video, a few more tapes and the corporate overview. He follows-up with another call three days after the package is sent.

This was Neil's response on why he prefers to mail the prospect a package of information:

"Most of my prospects are busy successful business people. By sending them a package, I have set up an easy to duplicate system that allows them to impart all the information needed without spending a lot of their own physical time. It limits face-to-face meetings to those prospects who are serious about joining the business."

(D) **The fourth option is to use an event:** Invite your prospect to an event. The most common event would be a local business briefing. It is much better to meet with a prospect prior to bringing them to a meeting. The chances that they will come to the meeting are much higher when you have established a personal relationship. If you meet them for the first time at the meeting you may be distracted with other prospects or distributors and you may not be able to give them the personal time and attention you should.

You have followed up with your prospect. You know their level of interest. You have met with them in a one-on-one or preferably in a two-on-one presentation or you sent them additional information. You have involved them in a three-way call. The next step is to get them to an event such as a local business meeting, a regional conference, a regional training school, a leadership conference, a corporate conference or a corporate tour. These events build and strengthen belief.

Once you sponsor someone into the business, you want to continue to promote events. Get your new distributor to the next corporate conference. Get them to a corporate tour as soon as possible. When their belief bucket is full, when they have that unshakeable belief in where they're going, they will not buy anyone else's story. They know deep down what's going on and they have absolute certainty that they are in the right vehicle. That's when they get good at attracting other people. That is when they are ready and willing to talk to the best people and brightest people they know.

You enter this business on faith that everything you have been told is true. You believe that the products are as good as we say they are, that the company is as good as we say it is and that the opportunity is the best in the land. Ultimately that faith turns to belief through participation, through using the products, being at the events and experience in the business. Your belief bucket needs to be constantly filled. All belief buckets come with a design defect, a small hole in the bottom. Over time your belief level and your enthusiasm drops. You can never stop filling your belief bucket through listening to Rexall Showcase International tapes and being at every event.

I Can't

John, I've talked to a lot of people and given them the tape. They like the tape, we sit down and talk and they walk away saying, "It sounds good but I can't do the business." What do you say to someone like that?

When someone says, "I can't do the business" challenge them, "Let's be honest with each other. Everyone can do the business and you can do the business. What you're saying is that you don't want to do the business. In our business there is no such thing as can't. We can all do it; it's just a matter of want to."

In many cases the individual does not have a strong enough "WHY". The very first question I always ask an interested prospect is,

"If you were to do the business, why would you do it?" If the individual does not have a WHY, you might as well move on.

Ask your prospect what their WHY is. If their "why" is to make a lot of money, tell them that it's not enough to say, "I want to make a lot of money". They need to put a specific figure down on paper. This is still not specific enough. Your next question should be, "If you were to earn this amount of money what would you do with it? How would it change your life?"

This is a good exercise for us to go through several times a day, sit back with your eyes closed and picture what your life will be like when you arrive, when you achieve your WHY. When you actually get there it will be like déjà-vu because you've lived it over and over in your mind and it will seem so familiar.

I'll give you a quick example to expand on this. At my second corporate conference a guy walked across the stage as a Triple Diamond. I will never forget what he said; "I was a Triple Diamond the day I signed up. It just took awhile for the paperwork to catch up." That's the attitude. That's the winning attitude.

On the horizon: "In a recent conversation with Doug Overvold we discussed things on the horizon such as E-commerce that may significantly enhance the way we communicate with people. The interesting thing is that this trend may empower an average communicator"

It is not a question of, "Will you get
knocked down?"
You will get knocked down, the question is
"Will you stay down?"

Product

"Let me try the product and then I'll think about doing the business." John, this is one of the most frequent responses I get. How would you respond?

This is probably the most frequent response we experience in the business. It is important to help people understand that our products are not on trial. Of course we want people to use our products, but not to see if the products work. The products work, they do what we say they will do. The objective in using products is to find out what works for you and to become familiar with the rest. A product does not have the same effect on everyone who uses it.

Let's look at a few examples: People will say, "If these products work, then I'll be all over It.". My response is, "Well, what happens if they don't work for you? Nothing works for everybody. It does not invalidate the opportunity just because it doesn't work for you." The question is "Does it work for most people?". That's what you need to know. This is a marketing opportunity."

Given our array of products, it would be almost impossible not to find at least one product that will have a positive impact on your health. Our real product is the opportunity, we are selling hope. We're giving people a chance to free themselves from dead-end jobs.

Another thing I'll say, "Do you think it's fair to conduct a one-person study to validate a product's effectiveness?" Who could say "yes" to that? Of course it's not fair, but that's what they're talking about doing. The key is not if it works for you, then you'll do the business. The key is "Does it work for most?" That is the real the issue.

Another example is a meeting I ran in Minneapolis with 75 to 100 people in the room. I did a question-and-answer session after the meeting. The very first question was a guy who laid out a five-minute dossier on his background, his degrees, positions and accomplishments before he got to his question. This was one very skeptical person. He asked, "How do I know this stuff isn't snake oil? How do I know it really works?" In essence he was saying, "Where's the proof?" I replied, "The proof is all around you. We just did a meeting and two-thirds of the people in this room stood up and gave testimonies on how the products have positively affected their lives." "I want to see the results" he stated, "I want to see the documentation." I said, "We have documentation and studies, but remember that there is no study, no article that is more powerful than someone having a personal experience." I paused, "Let me ask you a question. Let's just say that you tried our product and had tremendous results. It lowered your cholesterol and you never felt better. Someone produces a study that says it doesn't work. What are you going to do? Are you going to quit taking the product? If it works for you do you care what the study says?"

How many pharmaceutical products offer a 100% money back guarantee?

You will always be faced with people who want more information. They will say, "I want to see the studies, I want to see the documentation" Tell them, "I can produce the information you're looking for, but what then? Are we going to do business?" In many cases you can give them everything they ask for and they will still say no. My favorite question is "If this stuff is all that I say it is, and I can prove it, are we going to do business?" Get the yes before you do go through all the work of getting them the information.

Don't Babble

This is an area that I really caution people on. This is a very, very common error with new distributors. We are so excited with the business, the products, our new vision, the compensation plan, the management team, and the stock plan that we talk too much. In fact we babble.

We can do this in every phase in the business whether it's giving out an audiotape and blowing it by telling the whole story or talking too much on a three- way call when we're supposed to listen or overloading a poor prospect at a one-on-one presentation.

They say that 70% of communication is listening. Remember this the next time you get off on some long-winded explanation of the business, the one who does all the talking, is the one who loses.

Say less to more people. Put this on a 3 x 5 card. Put it on your day timer. Put it on the dashboard in your car. Write it on your mirror. Keep it in front of you. Say less to more people. Stop talking before your finished.

No Jargon

One of the first habits we fall into in network marketing is using the jargon of the industry. Upline, downline, crossline, sponsor, PV (personal volume), group, level, organization all mean little or nothing to a prospect. Using jargon can only confuse a prospect. If your prospect is confused he or she will never join you in the business.

Whoever does all the talking, loses.

Excuses

When I was building my NSA business I was driving from my hometown of Perham to Fargo every morning, an hour-and-a-half drive. I was the first one to open the door in the morning and the last one to leave at night. I was working with a young guy who was very enthusiastic. He lived on the other side of Fargo. Now the other side of Fargo is not like the other side of a major city, we're talking 10 to 15 minutes on a bad day. He was complaining to me about having to drive across town. Here I am driving 70 miles to be there early in the morning, every morning regardless of the weather and he's complaining about driving across town.

It amazes me when people say they want something and then they make excuses on why they can't get it. When your heart's not in it any excuse will do. It's like the person who asked his neighbor to borrow the lawn mower. The neighbor said, "No, I'm sorry; you can't borrow my lawn mower. My wife's making beef stroganoff." He asked, "What does beef stroganoff have to do with me borrowing your lawn mower?" The neighbor responded, "Listen, if I don't want to lend you my lawn mower, one excuse is as good as another."

Some people look for an excuse. A winner looks at every problem as a challenge. They find a way around it, through it or over it. It gets under my skin to see people complain about little things that in the big scheme of life mean nothing at all.

Claire Roth has a saying that I love;

You can have reasons or results.
Reasons don't count, results don't lie.

"I have no money."

Occasionally, you're going to run into people who say, "I'm your person. I can do this business, but I have no money. I can't even do the $300 Associate level."

I am a very firm believer in where there's a will; there's a way. If you want to do something badly enough, you can figure out how to do it. I believe that if someone can't come up with the minimum investment of $300 they will never make it anyway.

Let me give you a quick example of this. "You're telling me that you can't come up $300 but you will work your tail off, you would go after this and you would be my star." Let me ask you a question. "Let's say that when we're finished talking here today, you leave, and someone vandalized your car, they slit all four tires. What are you going to do? You're not going to walk everywhere you go. You're going to get new tires. Somehow you will find a way to buy those tires.

Here's the good news; your tires are fine. Wherever you would have found the money to buy those tires, do it now so that you can get started with Rexall Showcase International."

If the desire is strong enough,
you can always find a way.

For every discipline there is a multiple reward.
Every discipline affects every other discipline.
Discipline is the requirement for progress.
When you set up disciplines that give your life
structure miracles can happen – multiplied.
The most valuable disciplines are the
disciplines you impose on yourself.
Value is the fruitful result of discipline not hope.
Jim Rohn on discipline

CHAPTER 13

Why Rexall Showcase International?

There are five elements that make up a successful network-marketing venture. If you look at these five areas when choosing a company and if you're fair about it, you're going to make the choice that's right for you. I believe it is a mistake to select a company based on a product, an individual, a compensation plan, or any one or two attractive features of an opportunity. When you look at these five areas you will see that many companies will have two or three of them in place. You can make money with a company that has two or three of them in place, but if your goals are significant, you must have these five elements in place.

Number 1 is the company:. Is it a solid company? Rexall Sundown, as a publicly owned and publicly traded company makes it easy to get the whole story and to get the numbers behind the story. When a company is not publicly traded you have to accept whatever you're told. How long has the company been around? How good is the management team? What is their track record of success?

One thing RSI offers that no other company can match is a name that opens doors. By far the biggest challenge we face is overcoming the negative image of network marketing. A very good communicator can overcome this challenge. But what makes up the majority of every organization? The problem is that most organizations consist of average or poor communicators. The "Rexall" name gives every distributor a significant edge.

Number 2 is the products: Are they affordable, highly consumable, unique? Are the products mainline or are they the gimmicky or faddy type? Do people use them just because they're in the business? Do the products make sense? Rexall Showcase International sells products that are affordable, highly consumable and address huge market concerns. In many cases they are not just unique they are proprietary and contain patented formulations. They are mainline products. The need for more fiber in our diets is a well known, scientifically proven fact. Homeopathic products have been used for hundreds of years in Europe and Asia.

Number 3 is the compensation plan: A compensation plan must have provisions for a part-time person with reasonable effort to be fairly compensated. There must be provisions for career people; the heavy hitters to make big money, otherwise you're going to lose them. When these players realize how lucrative network marketing is they'll go to a company that's going to pay them.

The Rexall Showcase International compensation plan has some unique attributes. Our compensation plan makes it possible for the average person to access the money and at the same time it makes it possible to earn a significant income. I believe that Rexall Showcase International will produce the largest checks ever paid in network marketing.

Timing is the fourth element: Timing should be viewed on several fronts.

First is the timing of the industries we're involved in. Certainly, when you look at health care, at the size of the baby boom market with eleven thousand people a day turning fifty it is a huge and growing market. The good news is that it's going to continue for the next fifteen years. All these baby boomers grew up with Rexall. The Rexall name brings a warm, nostalgic memory of being young. They all want to look better, feel better and live longer.

The timing of this opportunity is important. As a company Rexall Showcase International is still small enough that an individual can get as much of this as they want and yet we're big enough that nobody can argue with our success. The timing today is certainly better now than when I got started. When I got started, there was no proof, we didn't know if Rexall Showcase International was going to make it. Today the proof is in our track record of success, in the products and in the money that's being made.

The last thing is the training and support: This should be looked at on a couple of fronts. The first is the caliber of people who are involved, the leadership, the training, and the people working with you. The way everyone works together is not the case in many companies. We all use the same training materials, the same approach, and the same presentation. The training materials provided by Rexall Showcase International and Sound Concepts are of high quality and affordable.

The company does not gouge its distributors with big markups on sales materials. The objective is to get sales support material into the hands of distributors for the lowest possible price so the distributors can get it out to prospects.

Look at these five areas – the company, the products, the timing, and the compensation, the training and support and rank each one on a scale of 1 to 10. This will help you make the right choice for you. Do you want to make an emotional decision or a business decision? Add up the points and go with the one that scores the highest. I'm confident you'll be with Rexall Showcase International.

The company:

The products:

The compensation:

Training and support:

Timing:

Does this look like a growth industry?

There are 44 million people over the age of 60, the largest segment of the population ever to be over 60. There are between 76 to 78 million people born between 1946 and 1964. These are the baby boomers, one third of the population jammed into about 19 years. These people make up the most significant buying segment of the population and they're more powerful than they have ever been before.

- They are healthier as a group than ever before.

- They are expected to live longer as a group than ever before.

- They have more money as a group than ever before.

- They have one common goal; they want to live longer and they want to live well longer. They are going to the health food stores spending their money to enhance their health and to prolong their lives.

- We sell into that marketplace.

Dollars spent on health compared to a 30-year-old:

- The average 50-year-old spends 4.5 times as much

- The average 60-year-old spends 7.0 times as much

- The average 65-year-old spends 9.5 times as much

From the tape "Options & Opinions" by Stewart Hughes and Randy Schroeder.

Live every day as if it were your last.
Marcus Aurelius

Sooner or later, those who win
are those who think they can.
Richard Bach

Any fact finding us is not as important
as our attitude toward it, for that
determines our success or failure.
Norman Vincent Peale

CHAPTER 14

Getting A New Distributor Started

John, imagine for a moment that you just signed me up on your front line, I'm brand new, I have absolutely no experience in network marketing. What do I have to do to be a successful as you've been in the business?

Be Coachable: There is a combination of things that we need to look at. Number 1 is to stress the importance of being coachable. Regardless of the success or failure you've had in the past, put them behind you. The people skills you've developed and your contacts will be valuable. No matter how successful you have been make a commitment to be coachable. I always ask for permission to give advice or to critique a new distributor if he or she is getting off track.

When Cliff, Doug and I signed up with Rexall Showcase International, Todd Smith was a tough coach. We listened, we followed Todd's advice and coaching. Sure we had been successful in other endeavors but this was a new deal and we were prepared to listen and to learn.

Get Your Why And Your Goals In Writing: The first rule of goal setting is that if your goals are not in writing, you don't have goals, you have dreams. Goals must be specific with definite deadlines. What are the action steps you must take to reach your WHY? When will you take each step? What will be done and when?

Make Your List: The next item is to write your list of prospective distributors. This will be your warm market, people with whom you have or had some kind of a relationship. Your warm market is anyone you can call and they recognize you. As you write your list do not prejudge anyone. We don't know who is at the right point in his or her life, and ready to do the business. Our responsibility is to get the information in front of everybody and then spend time with those who have an interest. You will find, as I did, that the people in whom you have the least expectations will be the best in the business.

Establish A Schedule: Decide and commit to how many hours a week you will work your Rexall business. Establish a work schedule in terms of what you will do on a day-to-day basis, the specific hours you will work and what you will do in those hours. How many tapes will you get into the mail, how many follow-up calls will you make? I hear people say, "I'm going to work this a couple of hours a day" and then they spend the first hour trying to figure out what they're going to do. A well-organized plan will help you to make much better use of the hours you put into your business.

Leaders are like eagles, they don't flock together,
you find them one at a time.

The 48-Hour Meeting: I believe that it is mandatory to meet with a new distributor within 48 hours of them signing up. Take enough time to work with them to get their goals in writing, to get them started on their list and to establish the schedule they intend to work. When you invest this time with a new distributor you are laying the foundations of their success.

Don't Sweat the Small Stuff: Don't get hung up on all the details of the business. To get started you do not have to understand every nuance of the compensation plan, you do not have to know every product, and how it works and what the ingredients are. You learn everything you need to know about network marketing in kindergarten, its called "Show and Tell." Your job is to tell the story.

Develop Your Story: We are overpaid storytellers. You won't be overpaid through your first few months in the business. We tell stories about our company, our products, what's happened to us and what's happened to others in the business. Develop your own story. What was it that attracted you to the business, how did you get started, what happened with some of the people that you brought into the business, how do you feel about what you're doing, would you ever go back to your old way of life? Keep it simple and keep telling the story.

Make Commitments: If you plan to be successful as a Rexall Showcase International distributor you must make serious commitments to your long-term success.

Don't sweat the small stuff, it's all small stuff.

The first commitment is a 90-day commitment that you'll do whatever it takes for the next 90 days to get this thing going. Get up an hour earlier or stay up an hour later, do whatever it takes to get your business off the ground. This business is like a big flywheel; you've got to keep cranking on it until it's spinning. Once it's spinning all you have to do is tap it occasionally.

Imagine an aeroplane heading down the runway. This plane lifts off at 100 mph. What happens if you go 90 mph? Nothing, it does not get off the ground. You could taxi from here to Fargo and you would not get off the ground. Once you take off it takes much less energy to keep the plane in the air that it took to get it off the ground. It's the same thing in this business. Your runway is 90 days. Do whatever it takes to get lift off, to get off the ground. Put the throttle to the wall.

Once you achieve lift off, you can back off a little on the throttle because you have other people supporting you, building their organizations and yours. Your business will take less energy to maintain that it took to get started but you can't take your eye off the ball. If you do it will roll right back on you.

You must commit to the long term. If you were to buy a franchise or start a traditional business how long would you expect it to take to break even? How long would you expect it to take before it started making a profit? If you invested $250,000 in a fast food franchise would you close the doors if a customer said no? Would you quit if you had a

Fast tempo is essential for success.
Fast is good, faster is better.
Brian Tracy

bad day? Would you close the doors if your number one, key manager quit? Rexall Showcase International is no different, like any business it will take time, hard work and plenty of sacrifice. Make an unconditional commitment that you will be here one year from today. Make a conscious, definite, deliberate decision that you will work your business hard for a year and then you will examine your options.

If you have been in the business for one full year then make a conscious, definite, deliberate decision that you will be doing this business for the next five years.

Become A Student of the Industry: I would strongly encourage you to become a student of the network marketing industry. The "Wave 3" book is excellent, I have it on tape. Our book, the Rexall story, Prescription for Success is a must read. There are many, many books and tapes that are generic to the industry. Mark Yarnell's books and tapes are excellent. His book and tapes; Your First Year in Network Marketing is a classic. Without question, I would want you to get into the self-development materials mentioned in this book. Make a commitment to work harder on yourself than you do on your business.

*These materials can be purchased at buymlmtools.com

To have a dynamic growing organization be a dynamic growing leader.

On Being Coachable

Neil Roth one of my front-line leaders came from the top echelons of the pharmaceutical industry. He worked at companies such as Eckerd Drugs, Revco Drug Stores, Carls Drugs, Thrifty Drugs in senior management positions up to and including president. During his best years he was earning in excess of $300,000 a year plus stock options and all the other perks that go with the top job. You can imagine how receptive Neil was to advice from a former maintenance manager. Neil did it his way for three months and then one day I asked him if he wanted to keep on doing it his way or if he would like to make some money? He decided to follow the system and he has become a Double Diamond, Century Club Elect and one of my strongest leaders.

Sometimes I worry about him because he is so tough on his leaders. Neil's response is that he does not want them to make the same mistakes he made.

John I've already blown it:

You may be reading this and saying, "John, I've been in the business for more than 90 days. I have already ruined my 90-day story. I've been in Rexall Showcase International for six months, a year, two years, whatever the figure may be."

The key is this, you can always go back around and make another approach. You can always start a 90-day story. You can say, "On this date, I got a new understanding of what I needed to do and let me tell you what happened in the last 90 days. Up to this point I did not understand what was going on, I didn't understand what I needed to do, I had not made the commitment. On this date, I understood what I needed to do, I made the commitment and let me tell you what happened in the last 90 days."

Start over, make your 90-day commitment and I will see you - at the top.

This is Doug Overvold's 90-day plan. Use it for your next 90 days. Start all over again, put the throttle to the wall, hit the runway at full speed and make it happen.

Doug Overvold's 90-day plan

1. **Put your plan in writing:** Use the following format or create your own.

2. **Fill the pipeline:** The key to effective recruiting is to have several prospects looking at the business. Make at least 50 contacts a month if you are part time and 100 a month if you are full time. A contact can be through a tape, a face-to-face meeting, a CD business card or through the Internet.

   I commit to make _____ contacts this month.

3. **Create your chicken list:** This is a list of the most successful and respected people you know. To have a rapidly growing business, you must present RSI to your best and brightest acquaintances. Use your upline if you are at all tentative about prospecting your "chicken list"

   I commit to show this to the sharpest people I know and will meet in the next 90 days. Initial: _____

4. **Three-way calls are essential** toward building belief in your prospects. If you are not utilizing your upline to build belief and to show your prospects the support that will be available to them, you will fall far short of your goals and you will duplicate failure.

   I commit to the making ___ three-way calls per week.

5. **One-on-one, two-on-one presentations:** This business is about relationships and is most effectively communicated person-to-person.

   I commit to making _____ presentations each week.

6. **Private Small Group Presentations** (PSGP) may well be the most effective way to collectively build your business. It shows

your prospects that time and their lack of product and business knowledge should not stop them from getting started.

I commit to have _____ PSGP a month.

7. **Conference calls** are an effective tool to build belief in your prospects. This party validation is a powerful way to have the story presented and reinforced by knowledgeable professionals.

I will have ___ prospects a week on a conference call.

8. **Sponsoring ratio:** the success of your organization will correlate directly to your front-line sponsoring activity. Be the example to your organization.

1 new distributor a month keeps you in the hunt.
3 new distributors a month = emerging leadership

9. Build for events: To maintain momentum you must build for events. Business meetings, regional conferences and corporate conferences will show your prospects "who we are" as well as "where we are going".

I will be at the next corporate conference   _____
I will be at the next regional training meeting _____

10. **Submit your plan** to an upline leader who agrees to be your coach. Review your plan with your coach at least once a month and follow his or her advice.

I will review my plan with my coach once a month ____

11. **Review your plan daily:** You plan is your "how" to get to the "where" you want to be.

I will review my plan every day for 90 days. _____

Activity Monitor

Month	1	2	3
Contacts made	_____	_____	_____
Three way calls made	_____	_____	_____
Presentations	_____	_____	_____
Prospects on conference calls	_____	_____	_____
Small Group Presentations	_____	_____	_____
Meetings with guests	_____	_____	_____
New distributors enrolled	_____	_____	_____

I commit to following my 90-day plan and to be accountable and coachable. It is my responsibility to implement the activities that will build my organization.

12. **Fill your belief bucket:** Most belief buckets come with a small hole in the bottom and need to be constantly refilled. Listen to audiotapes, attend every meeting, every corporate event, listen in on the conference calls and listen to your upline. Keep that belief bucket full.

The price of success is hard work, dedication to the job at hand and the determination that whether we win or lose, we have applied the best of ourselves to the task at hand.

Vince Lombardi

Commitment

If it was easy would Rexall Showcase International pay 63 cents on the dollar in commissions?

Commitment is the backbone, the foundation of success in Rexall Showcase International. Commitment comes back to the fact that people buy people. People are not going to follow someone who is not committed. I'll give you a couple of examples.

I was in Minneapolis doing a two-on-one presentation with a brand new distributor and a prospect. I did the presentation and the prospect was very excited. The prospect looked over to the new distributor and said, "Well, Joe, this looks really good. What are you doing with it?" Joe replied, "Well, I'm between jobs. I thought I'd give it a try." You know what your response would be, "Try it on someone else, not me." People want to work with people who are committed, people who are focused and going places.

Another example is in your own workplace. You can tell the people who are committed to their company, who are there to do their job the best they can vs. those people who are there to pick up a pay check. No one has to tell you who is who, you can see it in his or her actions.

It's the same thing in this business. Commitment is very, very important. It is not easy to maintain your commitment when the tough times come, when you give out 25 tapes without a shred of interest, when the dream stealers get to you, when you keep investing time and money with no return. As Earl Nightingale says, "It's hard to pay the price when the picture isn't clear."

Suppose I guaranteed you $100,000. I put it in a bank account payable to you in 12 months. Your job is to get out three tapes a week, do three two-on-ones meetings a week and bring two people a week to a business presentation. Will you be committed? Without question, you would do it, you would be committed. You could see the picture, it would be crystal clear.

What if I told you that if you to do the same things you'll get double that, you'll get $200,000 but there is no guarantee. It will be more difficult for you because the picture isn't quite as clear.

Belief builds commitment: Not everybody is going to buy your story. The important thing is that you don't buy their story about why it won't work. I remember trying to recruit an old friend in my hometown. He was completely negative. He gave me every reason in the world why this would not work, "The Japanese will come out with it and you guys will be all done." He had a list of reasons a mile long . I finally shut him up by saying, "If you were around back when Thomas Edison was working on the light bulb you would have talked him out of it and we would all be reading in candlelight." I finally told him, "Even if it ended tomorrow, I'd be a million dollars ahead of you."

Don't expect everybody to believe your story. The important thing is don't let them convince you that their story has merit. One of the reasons that our opportunity is so lucrative is because most people will not see it.

If it's hard, then do it hard.
Les Brown

I Feel Like Quitting

John we all get discouraged in this business, did you ever reach a point when you wanted to quit and, just chuck the whole thing in?

We all have good days and bad days. I always tell people, "A bad day in Rexall Showcase International is better than a good day at work." But still, we all get frustrated and entertain the idea of quitting. We are going to have our down days, it comes with the territory. Anybody who would tell you that they never felt like quitting is not being honest with himself or herself or with you. Even Todd Smith had days when he felt like quitting. We all wonder if we have the strength, the endurance, the belief, and the patience to keep on keeping on.

I do a couple things. First I look at the alternatives. In the real world I'm worth about $10 an hour. I would have to be at work by 8:00 every morning and many evenings I would still be working at 7:00 or 8:00 or later. I would be on call 24 hours a day, 7 days a week. I would see much less of my family. Look at your own alternatives, would you want to go back to your prior occupation? If you're doing RSI part time, do you want to be totally dependent on your current time job for the rest of your life? Do you want your destiny to be in the hands of someone else who can tell you good-bye at the drop of a hat?

The next thing I do is get back into my Rexall tapes and my motivational tapes. The cure for 'stinkin thinkin' is to go back to putting the good stuff in. If you keep putting the good stuff in your whole attitude will change.

A bad day as a Rexall Showcase Distributor is better than a good day at work.

One of the biggest challenges we face in building our Rexall Showcase International business is ourselves. The challenge is working on ourselves to stay positive, focused, motivated and disciplined. Ultimately our success is up to us. Success is an inside job.

The other thing is to review your goals and remind yourself of your "why". This by itself can be a very motivating exercise. Remind yourself that if you're not going to follow through, if you quit you will have to give up all your goals. "I guess we're not going to have a new house, I'm not going to get the new car, I'm not going to have a retirement fund. The kids won't be able to go to college." Keep your "why" out in front of you. It will keep you focused and keep you going.

When you feel like quitting look at your alternatives, listen to your Rexall tapes, refocus on your why, review your goals and get focused. This is how you will separate yourself from the pack, from the mass of people who lead lives of quiet desperation. If you feel like quitting, you're normal, just don't quit.

Would you have given a tape to these individuals?

Would you have put this guy on your list? Would you have expected him to do well as a Rexall Showcase International distributor? He is a maintenance manager with a self-esteem so low that when you pass him in the hall he does not lift up his head to say hello unless you speak first. When you see him he is dressed in dark blue work clothes covered with grease. His favorite activity is maintaining and building equipment. He spends his time with his buddies down at the local pub, in the fish house or hunting. Oh, by the way, he lives in a trailer park, how many people can he know?

How about this guy? He owns several insurance agencies, a car wash and a string of fast food franchises. He is obviously a very successful individual. Ask Rick Jordan if he appreciates that a client literally coerced him to come to a network marketing opportunity meeting.

How about this guy? At one point you would have said, "He has too much money, he is not a prospect." Later in the same year you would have said, "He can't afford it, he's too broke". As Randy Schroeder says, "Both these statements were true, nobody thought that I was a good prospect, nobody approached me, that was a mistake, they should have approached me".

How about Carol? She is one of those artists, earning less than $12,000 a year as a sign painter. The next time Carol does one of her Saturday morning training sessions be sure to dial in. Ask Carol Evenson about setting goals.

There is no courage without fear.

How about an attorney, a very successful tax attorney, accountant and entrepreneur earning a six-figure income? One day Carol summoned up her courage and gave David Bailly a tape. Today David still runs a very successful practice, he is a leader in Rexall Showcase International, he is a member of the Century Club and Carol earns more in a month than she did in a year.

Now here is an individual who would never be interested in network marketing. He owns the largest Cadillac dealership from Minnesota to the West Coast. When he was asked to watch a network marketing video by his son he locked his office door and closed all the blinds so that no one would see him watching it. Today Cliff Overvold is one of Rexall Showcase International's top earning leaders.

How about a very successful real estate and property developer in the throes of a business failure, forced to file for bankruptcy. With a major loss like this behind him there is no way Eddie Stone would be interested in a preventative health care company, is there?

Would you approach a doctor who was a Founding Fellow of the American Rheumatology Association, a former director of Residency Training and Postgraduate Education at the Atlanta Hospital, Board Certified in Foot and Ankle Surgery, a former clinical instructor of Medicine at Emory University School of Medicine, and a Fellow of the American College of Foot and Ankle surgery? Dr. Lou Pack would never be interested in natural products as a better quality of care for his patients and getting himself out of the Rat Race, would he?

The next time you're feeling intimidated remember:

You miss 100% of the shots you don't take.
Wayne Gretsky

Quitting

We all feel like quitting, its normal.

- The key is, winners don't quit.

- Winners dig deep down inside themselves.

- Winners remind themselves where they came from and where they're going.

- Winners re-examine their goals.

- Winners make new plans.

- Winners make just one more phone call, give out just one more tape, attend just one more meeting, talk to their upline just one more time.

- Winners pass on some encouragement to someone in their downline.

- Before they know it winners are back on track.

Finding your pearls:

How many people will you have to approach to find your key leaders who will follow through and build the business? I don't know. This business is like a big bucket of oysters; you have to keep  shucking the oysters until you find the pearls. Sometimes you find them at the top of the bucket, sometimes in the middle, sometimes at the bottom, occasionally you have to get another bucket.

I can promise you this, the pearls are there, they are always there. I have never met anyone who has failed in our business. I know a lot of people who have quit, but I have never met anyone who has failed. If you stay the course, if you continue shucking oysters, you're going to find your pearls.

Success is a journey, not a destination.
Enjoy the journey.

The journey is the reward.

The rewards always come in the second mile.

Are you making a living or designing a life?
Anthony Robbins

The Journey Continues

Adversity reveals genius.

Horace

Even if you're on the right track, you'll

get run over if you just sit there.

Will Rogers

Live your beliefs and you can turn

the world around.

Henry David Thoreau

CHAPTER 15

Rewards of the Journey

John sometimes I just want to go back to some nice safe 9:00 to 5:00 job with a regular paycheck every week. Tell me again what happens if I just keep on keeping on.

What happens when you focus on your dream, when you move through the rejections, the sacrifices, the early years of just getting by? What happens when you overcome the negative self-talk, slip quietly around the dream-stealers and just keep on keeping on?

You arrive at the lifestyle you imagined for yourself. In fact network marketing can change your life in ways that are beyond your imagination. What have you envisioned for yourself? All of these things are possible for you. If others have done it, can you do it? If I did it can you do it?

Personal Freedom: You can attain personal freedom with no company to work for, no boss to answer to, no customers to jump for and no clients to please.

Financial freedom: You can have money in the bank and every debt paid in full. You can have investments, a house that is mortgage free and cars that are yours, 100% yours.

* Please note: In my opinion these rewards are all possible. They are not guaranteed and these statements are not intended to infer that they are guaranteed.

Is there any profession in the world
where you can put your family first?

Family: You can put your family first and work your schedule around your family so that you are at every event. When other parents are putting in overtime, you're there at the little league baseball game cheering your kids on. Do you think they will remember this? Instead of being stuck at the office, you can be there when your family needs you. When your son or daughter has the flu, you're there to bring them chicken soup.

Travel: There comes a point in our business when the world is your playground. You can travel to any place, at any time and not be concerned about the money or the time you are taking from your business. When you get home there will be no emergencies to deal with; no panic calls that only you can fix. There may, however, be a larger paycheck than the one you received the month before you took off.

Recognition: One of our deepest needs is the hunger for recognition, to be acknowledged for our contributions. There is no place like network marketing for recognition. When we think of recognition we think of the public, on-stage events that celebrate major milestones on our journey. Recognition comes from many other sources in network marketing. The most meaningful recognition is to see one of your distributors using your advice and training to accomplish his or her goals. When one of your distributors sees his or her dream becoming reality the satisfaction cannot compete with any form of public recognition. There is also a quiet personal satisfaction as you move through major milestones and on top of all that is the appreciation from product users as they see significant changes in their health and well being.

Network marketing can change your life in ways that are beyond your imagination.

Circle of friends: Would you like to have a circle of friends who were relentlessly upbeat, always positive, always focused on growing and helping others to grow? This is the kind of people you will be with and grow with in Rexall Showcase International.

My own example: Does it get any better than this?

In my case I am able to spend my summers and every weekend all year at my lake home in Minnesota. I work at my lake home and at the same time I am able to spend a large part of every day with my family.

I have friends in 50 states and four countries. With a phone call I will be picked up at any major airport in the country and treated like a visiting celebrity.

My income is in the top one/tenth of one percent of the top earners in North America. Money is no longer a major consideration in my life. The news that one of my leaders has qualified for the Century

Club means more to me today than my next paycheck, regardless how big it may be.

Most meaningful is the personal freedom I have to do what I want to do, with whom I want to do it, when I want to do it and where I want to do it. I associate with people I enjoy being with from both a business and a social perspective.

One of the most significant rewards of network marketing is the quality of life that it has made possible for me, particularly the amount of time I can spend with my family and children.

As I was leaving on one of my trips my youngest daughter Nicole asked, "dad do you have to go?' my oldest daughter Stephanie said "Nicole we get to see our dad way more than anyone else gets to see their dad".

The Unique Attributes of the RSI Business

In his tape "The Unique Attributes of the RSI Business", Tom Bissmeyer describes an idyllic family setting. Tom says, "Have you ever had an experience where you suddenly realized you were living your dream and you wanted to freeze the world and stay like that forever?

"The other night ... I'm in my home office and what was going on was one of those experiences. You see I got into this business to be around my family.   I was travelling 250 days a year and missing everything. As I'm sitting there doing a three way phone call, my wife is on my computer doing some E-mail to her friends. My daughter is sitting at my desk doing her homework. My little boy is standing on a chair scribbling on my white board drawing a bunch of funny colors. The dog's lying next to the fireplace and I'm doing a three way phone call."

"I asked myself, 'What other business would allow you to experience this?' We were all doing our own thing and yet we were together, how neat."

This lifestyle is within your reach. The question is "How much do you want it?"

Network marketing is not a job; it is a lifestyle.
Network marketing is simply a better way to live.
Randy Schroeder

Destiny is not a matter of chance;
it is a matter of choice.
It is not a thing to be waited for;
it is a thing to be achieved.
William Jennings Bryan

CHAPTER 16

Where do we go from Here?

In his book Wave 3 and now Wave 4 Richard Poe stresses the importance of technology in the astounding growth of network marketing over the last ten years. Technology makes it possible for a customer in California to place an order with a company in Florida and have the product on her doorstep within 24 hours. The distributor in New Hampshire sees a commission for this sale on her next statement. The computer calculates the commissions six levels up from the distributor, pays commissions and bonuses as appropriate and makes sure that each distributor receives the correct PV (personal volume). The computer calculates the freight due, the taxes owing, collects the taxes, forwards them to the correct agency, does the accounting, relieves the inventory and includes the latest product bulletin in the shipment.

That same distributor can now contact everyone in her organization through a telephone hook-up that allows her to broadcast a message to all

23,000 people in her organization, to her key 100 distributors or to her 7 front line leaders. Ten years ago it would have taken weeks to get a message like this out. You can imagine how the message would have changed by the time it reached the very last person in her organization and you can imagine how many question and clarification calls would have been required.

The Internet:

And then the Internet appeared on the scene. All of the above has happened without the Internet. Web pages are already in the process of taking network marketing to an entirely new level.

Training: Imagine sitting in your living room doing a business meeting in all 50 states and as many countries as you can imagine. There is absolutely no limit to the number of distributors and prospects who could be in on this business meeting. It could be a meeting with live interaction from the distributors or it could have been taped for broadcast. Every distributor hears the exact same story from an accomplished professional such as Todd Smith, Randy Schroeder, Stewart Hughes or any of the leaders in Rexall Showcase International.

Company news: Company news including product announcements, business plan updates, special contests and upcoming events can be broadcast to hundreds or thousands of people simultaneously for pennies.

High tech and high touch: Ease of use will make the Internet as familiar as a telephone. We will communicate to entire groups or one-on-one to anyone, anywhere in the world, in real time, for pennies a minute.

Rexall Showcase International: Rexall Showcase International has made a commitment to be on the leading edge of this technology.

Today we can enter an order, register a new distributor, check on the status of an order and check our volumes instantly. A prospect can access a great deal of information about the company and its products from the comfort of home at his or her convenience.

Compact Discs (CD's)

Compact Discs (CD's) will be a new and very powerful presentation tool as we move into the 2000's. For less than $5.00 a CD can present the entire business on a computer screen or television screen.

Imagine a CD the size of a business card that combines both sight and sound. The viewer can point and click the topics he or she is interested in. The viewer can review the information as many times as they wish in the comfort of his or her own home. If a prospect comes close to the profile of a typical Rexall Showcase International Distributor it is virtually guaranteed that they will have some degree of familiarity with a computer. A CD is a leading edge medium that the prospect can load in his or her computer and review the information at his or her leisure. The response we will see from many prospects as they view our CD's is, "This is a good presentation, it is very simple, I can pass on a CD like this to my associates".

CD's can be updated quickly as new products are introduced. They can be used for training, recruiting and education. They are convenient, you can carry a business card CD in your shirt pocket, and they are inexpensive.

Our world is changing ...... *fast*

It is important for us as Rexall Showcase International Independent Distributors to stay on top of our rapidly changing industry. The audiotape which has served us so well over the past years may give way to other approaches such as the CD business card, discussions through the Internet, opportunity meetings on the Internet, E-Commerce and e-mail.

Our objective is to get the RSI story in front of as many people as possible and to get it to them through the most appropriate medium. We may tell the story face-to-face in a one-on-one meeting or in a two-on-one meeting, or with a CD business card, or with an audiotape, or with a videotape, or through our Web pages or at an event. The important thing is that the story is told.

In the prospecting stage network marketing is a numbers game. It takes big numbers to find your leaders. It becomes a relationship game as you work with your distributors and your leaders to assist them in building their business.

These new tools will give us a tremendous advantage in contacting large numbers of prospects and in communicating with our distributors.

A new approach to Team Building
Time Vs Tools

As this book goes to print a new Team Building Book and new approaches to the business have just been introduced. Audiotapes have been a very successful program for the past seven years and they will continue to be a key component of team building. The new Team Building Book will introduces additional approaches to recruiting.

As a Rexall Showcase International Independent Distributor you will invest time or tools or a combination of both to build your organization. In the past we have placed a great deal of emphasis on tools, audiotapes and videotapes. The new Team Building approach suggests that there are situations where time is a more effective investment than tools.

There are many individuals within our circle of acquaintances who would rather meet for a cup of coffee or lunch than listen to a tape. They are more receptive to a face-to-face discussion than to listening to a stranger on a tape. These same individuals may prefer the dynamics of a meeting to watching videotape.

The new Team Building Book is one more step in the on-going evolution of our profession. Rexall Showcase International has a track record of being on the leading edge of this evolution.

Nothing splendid has ever been achieved except by those who believed that something inside of them was superior to circumstances.

Bruce Barton

CHAPTER 17

Where do YOU
go from here?

If you're not on board with Rexall Showcase International yet this is the industry, the company and the products that will assist you in making your dream your reality. Network marketing is far more than any job, it is a way of life. It can change your life in ways that are beyond your imagination. As a maintenance manager, do you think I ever imagined having my story told in a book like this, earning a six figure income, having friends in 50 states and four countries or having my own video and audio tapes? Rexall Showcase International changed my life. It can change yours if you follow the system.

*Execution is everything, having just a
vision is no solution, everything
depends on execution.*
Brian Tracy

We are positioned at the convergence of four major trends. These trends are in the process of changing not just the way we do business but the way we live.

The Baby Boomers: Over 11,000 people a day are turning 50. These baby boomers grew up with Rexall. They want to look better, feel better and live longer. This baby boom generation has driven every market they encountered from the baby food industry through real estate. Two industries are being transformed by this generation, the financial markets and preventative health care. Our products fit this generation like a hand in a glove.

Home Based Business: Ten years ago if you told a friend that you were working from home, he or she would have expressed their condolences, "I'm sorry to hear that you have come to that". Today a home based business is viewed as 'a better quality of life' and we are just on the leading edge of this wave. Today we can run multi-million dollar organizaitons from home with a phone and a fax.

E-Commerce: Futurists claim that over the next five years E-Commerce will change our lives more than the change we have seen in the last 50 years. Every Director in Rexall can set up their own web page with links to our leading edge Rexall Showcase International web site.

International Markets: Business knows no boundaries. The introduction of E-Commerce and the leap in communication technology makes it possible for a major international corporation to do business around the world. This same technology is available to us as RSI distributors. We have a seamless network-marketing plan that makes it as easy to sponsor a new distributor in Hong Kong as across the street.

The difference between success and failure is the ability to take action. As Anthony Robbins says, "Personal power is the ability to take action".

What if these trends are changing our world?

What if this business can change your life?

What if you miss it?

Your first few steps: The first steps are to sign your distributor agreement, order your products, select your tapes from Sound Concepts, get your goals on paper, write your warm list and start exposing people to the opportunity. The good news is that you have a proven system to follow along with the best training and support in the industry. The bad news is that its easy not to, its easy to stay where you are and keep doing what you're doing.

Ask yourself this question 'If I keep on doing what I'm doing will it make my dream my reality?"

If you have been a Rexall Distributor for awhile this is the time to set new goals, to raise your sights and to rededicate yourself. Why not start all over again with your own 90-day plan?

"What lies behind you, and what lies ahead of you is of very little importance when compared with what lies within you."
Oliver Wendel Holmes

These are my goals for the next 90 days.

I will spend _____ minutes a day on self-development.

I will allocate these times every day to self-development.

From _____ to _____.

I will get _____ tapes out every day.

I will make _____ follow-up calls a day.

I will spend _____ a day on my business.

I will allocate this time to my business.

Monday   From _____ to _____

Tuesday   From _____ to _____

Wednesday   From _____ to _____

Thursday   From _____ to _____

Friday   From _____ to _____

Saturday   From _____ to _____

Sunday evening is the best time for follow-up calls.

I will be at the next Rexall Showcase International convention in

_____

What will I do differently for the next 90 days?

_____

_____

_____

_____

_____

_____

_____

_____

_____

_____

_____

_____

_____

An Old Fable

Brian Tracy tells an old fable on one of his tapes.

Many years ago, in ancient Greece, a traveller met an old man on the road and asked him how to get to Mount Olympus. The old man, who happened to be Socrates, replied by saying, "If you really want to get to Mount Olympus, just make sure that every step you take is in that direction."

The moral of the fable is simple. If you want to be successful, if you want to see your dream become your reality be sure that *every step you take is in that direction*.

Take your first step now and I will see you at the top of the mountain.

You will see me at the top of the mountain or
you will find me dead along the side.
You will not find me at the bottom of the mountain.

John Haremza

These are the tape sets that I have found to be the most valuable in my own personal growth.

Zig Ziglar

Goal Setting Program

Developing the Qualities of Success

Jim Rohn

The Art of Exceptional Living

Challenge to Succeed in the 90's

Making of a Leader for the 90's, Volume 1

Making of a Leader for the 90's, Volume 2

The Power of Ambition

Take Charge of Your Life

Earl Nightingale

Lead the Field

The Strangest Secret

Communicating What You Think

Brian Tracy

Getting Rich in America

The Luck Factor

The Psychology of Success

The Science of Self-Confidence

Stephen Covey

The Seven Habits of Highly Effective People

Living the Seven Habits

First Things First

Napolean Hill

Think and Grow Rich

Dennis Waitley

Seeds of Greatness

Bob Proctor

The Success Puzzle

Lou Tice

Mastering the Attitude of Achievement

These tapes can be purchased at www.buymlmtools.com